Louise Davies left King's College of Household and Social
Science (now Queen Elizabeth College, London University)
with a B.Sc. degree and a conviction that scientists need
interpreting. She has therefore combined the study of
nutrition with writing, broadcasting, interviewing, lecturing
and television appearances. At the Ministry of Food she
wrote a monthly magazine, *Food and Nutrition*, for dieticians
and domestic science teachers and managed to involve the
whole school curriculum with the subjects. Her first book,
See How to Cook, was a pioneer in picture cookery books.
For twelve years she broadcast 'Shopping List' twice weekly in
the B.B.C. *Today* programme, giving advice on shopping and
recipe hints, and combining this and other broadcasts with
a busy home life. Now, as head of the Geriatric Nutrition
Unit at Queen Elizabeth College, she is conducting research
into the nutritional needs of the elderly and is actively
encouraging practical help for those who shop for one or
two. Louise Davies is her maiden name. She is a widow with
two daughters. Her book *Easy Cooking for One or Two* (1972)
has also been published in Penguins.

Easy Cooking
for Three or More

Louise Davies

ILLUSTRATED BY
Tony Odell

Penguin Books

Penguin Books Ltd,
Harmondsworth, Middlesex, England
Penguin Books Australia Ltd,
Ringwood, Victoria, Australia
Penguin Books Canada Ltd,
41 Steelcase Road West, Markham, Ontario, Canada
Penguin Books (N.Z.) Ltd,
182–190 Wairau Road, Auckland 10, New Zealand

First published 1975

Copyright © Louise Davies, 1975

Made and printed in Great Britain by
Hazell Watson & Viney Ltd, Aylesbury, Bucks
Set in Monotype Baskerville

For Paula and Ruth

Contents

Introduction

There are two kinds of cooks: those who only want to be told the rough idea and from there on prefer to use their own experience or to improvise; and those who follow a recipe faithfully. Both are catered for in this book. The basic idea is given at the beginning for the improvisers. Following this is the detailed step-by-step recipe.

Many of these recipes were first broadcast by me in 'Shopping List' in the B.B.C.'s *Today* programme, but were never published. 'Shopping List', originally scheduled for three months, ran for twelve years to an audience of over five million listeners at 7.30 a.m. and 8.30 a.m. every Wednesday (for the midweek shopping) and Friday (for catering at weekends). During that time I broadcast an average of two 'quick-change' recipes a week. This is the pick of the bunch, now updated with some altogether new recipes, plus hints for freezer owners.

Why were they called 'quick-change'? I felt that most families enjoy familiar recipes for everyday eating – and some husbands and children positively rebel against too much experimentation – but this makes it dull for the cook. So these dishes made a compromise: familiar roasts, grills, casseroles and desserts, but given an easy, quick change with unusual presentation or different flavourings.

Not all the recipes fall into this category. I could not omit many of our family favourites, like lemon meringue pie and potato and watercress soup. This is not a 'gimmicky' book, so I have included some well-known recipes that we especially enjoy cooking and eating.

I have not given metric amounts and centigrade temperatures because most British cooks have not yet converted their equipment and thinking to grammes and centigrade. But for those already using the new scales, there are conversion tables on pages 222–5.

This is not a book on food freezing but hints on freezing are included because more cooks are becoming freezer owners. They are finding that freezing is such a natural process that most normal recipes can be frozen at one stage or another in their preparation with satisfactory results, subject to a few general rules. It is assumed that freezer owners are already used to the basic methods and know their preferred ways and the equipment they need, so the notes in the recipes are for guidance only.

Most cakes, biscuits and bread freeze extremely well. They should be cooled before freezing, but not for too long (for instance 20–30 minutes' cooling is sufficient for a Victoria sandwich; other cakes and biscuits should just be cooled to room temperature before freezing). You may prefer to freeze some firm biscuit mixtures uncooked, wrapped in a sausage shape (see details under Re-

3 De-rind the bacon and remove any small bones. Flatten the bacon with a knife and cut each rasher across in two, to the length of the sausages.

4 Place the bacon on the pastry, spread the rashers with French mustard. Place a sausage on each rasher.

5 Damp the edge of the pastry and roll over, press and trim to make sausage rolls.

6 Brush with beaten egg, snip with scissors to decorate and bake at 400°F, gas mark 6, till golden and cooked through (about 20 minutes).

7 Serve hot or cold.

Sausage Kebabs

This is a simple kebab which needs no preliminary marinading. Merely skewer together sausages, bacon and pineapple and grill gently. Serve with hot rice and a salad, or with rice salad (page 141).

Serves 4

You will need 8 kebab skewers

INGREDIENTS

½ lb. chipolata sausages	oil
½ lb. back bacon	rice salad (page 141) or plain
1 small can pineapple slices	boiled rice and a salad

METHOD

1 Divide each sausage to form 3 miniature sausages by pressing gently and then twisting and cutting.

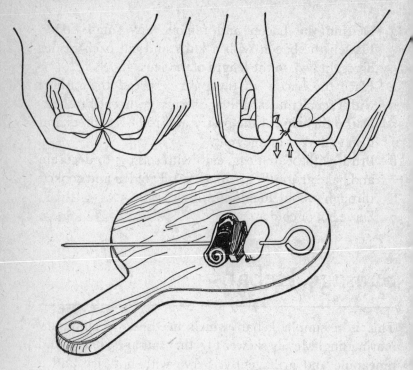

2 De-rind the bacon and cut it to a size which will form
   small rolls pinned onto the skewers.

3 Cut each pineapple slice into 8 wedges.

4 Skewer in turn a sausage, a bacon roll and a pineapple wedge and continue in that order until the
   skewer is filled – the pieces should be close together
   but not quite touching.

5 Brush lightly with oil, although this is not essential if
   the bacon is fatty.

6 Grill gently, turning once, till the sausages are well
   cooked – about 20 minutes.

7   Serve with hot plain rice and a salad or with rice
    salad (page 141).

Smoked Sausage and Vegetable Hot-Pot*

This is a Norwegian recipe called 'Lapskaus'. It is thick
with diced vegetables, soup and smoked sausage and is
a meal in itself.

Serves 8 – or 4 one day, re-heated for 4 the next

INGREDIENTS

1 lb. potatoes
1 lb. carrots
1 swede
1 small cauliflower
1 lb. leeks
2 pints water

1 beef or chicken stock cube
salt and pepper
2 smoked pork sausages
   (boiling ring), or 12
   frankfurters

METHOD

1   Prepare the vegetables by peeling if necessary and
    then dicing or slicing into small pieces.
2   Boil the prepared vegetables in the water and stock
    cube with seasoning to taste and continue to simmer
    until almost tender.

❋ Prepared stew/soup will freeze well, but I suggest adding
   frankfurters or boiling ring during re-heating.

3   Add the cut-up sausages and continue simmering
    until the vegetables are tender.
4   Serve hot, in soup plates.

Spaghetti with Ham*

To use up the remains of cooked ham economically, make
a quick version of Spaghetti Bolognese, using the cooked
ham in place of raw minced meat. After frying chopped
onion in oil till softened, add the cubed ham, canned
tomatoes with juice, tomato purée, dried basil and a lump
of sugar. Simmer well and serve this sauce over cooked
spaghetti. Sprinkle, if you like, with grated Parmesan
cheese.
Serves 4

INGREDIENTS

1–2 tablespoons olive oil   1 level teaspoon dried basil
1 small onion, chopped   1 lump (or half teaspoon)
approximately 6 oz. cooked   sugar
   ham, cut in small cubes   1 lb. spaghetti
1 (14-oz.) can peeled tomatoes   grated Parmesan cheese
2 teaspoons tomato purée   (optional)

METHOD

1   In a saucepan heat the oil and fry the onion till
    softened but not brown.

✱ The sauce may be frozen for 2 to 3 weeks and re-heated
   while spaghetti is cooking.

2 Add the ham, the tomatoes with juice, purée, basil and sugar. Simmer over a low heat for 20 to 30 minutes, stirring occasionally to break up the tomatoes.

3 Meanwhile cook the spaghetti in plenty of fast-boiling salted water until just soft enough to eat (generally this takes 15 to 20 minutes but some brands cook more quickly). Strain.

4 Pour the ham sauce over the spaghetti and sprinkle with grated Parmesan cheese if liked.

Worcestershire Sausage and Mash

Fry sausages slowly, without pricking, till thoroughly cooked through. Serve with creamy mashed potatoes, the flavour pepped up with Worcestershire sauce.

Serves 4

INGREDIENTS

lard
1 lb. sausages
2 lb. potatoes, peeled
milk

butter
pepper and salt
2–3 teaspoons Worcestershire sauce

METHOD

1 Melt enough lard to grease the bottom of a frying pan well.

2 *Over low heat* fry the unpricked sausages till thoroughly
   cooked (allow at least 20 minutes for pork sausages),
   turning them occasionally with kitchen tongs or two
   spoons. If you cook sausages slowly like this they
   should not burst but will cook right through and
   brown evenly.
3 Meanwhile boil the potatoes (cut up if necessary) and
   when they are cooked through mash them thoroughly,
   adding a little milk, a knob of butter and pepper and
   salt to taste.
4 When the potatoes are smooth and fluffy, mash in the
   Worcestershire sauce.
5 Serve the hot sausages on top of the hot mashed
   potatoes – a simple meal but warming and welcome
   on a cold day.

Chapter 5
Chicken

Chicken Cacciatore*

Frozen chicken quarters still offer good value for money. Thaw them well, fry them in butter, then serve them with an easily made sauce of onions, peppers, garlic and tomatoes.

Serves 4

INGREDIENTS

3 oz. butter
4 small chicken quarters
    (thawed)
1 large onion, chopped
1 medium green pepper,
    chopped
1 clove garlic, crushed

1 (16-oz.) can tomatoes
1 chicken stock cube
salt and pepper
½ teaspoon basil (optional), or
    1 teaspoon oregano
    (optional)
½ teaspoon sugar

✳ The advantage of a freezer is best employed here by storing the uncooked chicken joints before serving as suggested.

METHOD

1 Melt 2 oz. of the butter and fry the chicken quarters for 30 to 40 minutes or until thoroughly cooked through, turning occasionally during cooking.
2 Meanwhile, for the sauce, melt the remaining 1 oz. butter in a saucepan and fry the onion, green pepper and garlic together gently for 5 minutes.
3 Stir in the contents of the can of tomatoes, the crumbled stock cube, the seasonings, herbs and sugar. Bring to the boil, cover and simmer for 15 minutes.
4 Place cooked chicken in a heated serving dish, pour sauce over and serve.

Chicken with Herb Dumplings

Chicken pieces are simmered, but instead of using water and cut-up vegetables, substitute a packet of chicken vegetable soup and a small packet of frozen peas. About 25 minutes before serving, drop into the pan some dumplings to which dried marjoram or dried mixed herbs have been added.

Serves 6

INGREDIENTS

6 pieces chicken
1 packet chicken vegetable
  soup
1 small packet frozen peas
parsley to garnish

Dumplings
6 oz. self-raising flour
3 oz. shredded suet
1 level teaspoon salt
1 level teaspoon dried
  marjoram or mixed herbs

METHOD

1 Place the chicken in a saucepan with the reconstituted soup mix and water. Bring to the boil, cover, reduce the heat and simmer for 1 hour, stirring occasionally.
2 Stir in the peas.
3 Mix together the flour, suet, salt and marjoram or mixed herbs. Add sufficient water to make a soft dough. Divide into 6 equal portions and drop the dumplings into the stew. Cover again and cook for 25 minutes until the dumplings are light.

Chicken or Lamb Rice

This is a sort of paella. The onions and peppers are fried, washed rice and stock are added and cooked until the rice is tender. Then cut-up chicken or lamb, mushrooms and (optional) prawns or shrimps are heated up in the mixture, which is flavoured with ground cumin, oregano and lemon juice.

Serves 4

INGREDIENTS

4 tablespoons olive oil
1 large Spanish onion, chopped
1 large green pepper, chopped
6 tablespoons long-grain rice
1¼ pints stock

4 oz. mushrooms, sliced
diced cooked lamb or chicken
2 oz. shelled prawns or a small
  can of shrimps
  (optional)

1½ teaspoons ground cumin   1½ teaspoons oregano
   (optional)   juice of ⅛ lemon

METHOD

1   Heat the oil in a large frying pan. Fry the onion and
    pepper till soft.
2   Add the washed rice and fry for a few minutes.
3   Pour on the boiling stock and simmer, uncovered, for
    15 minutes.
4   Add the mushrooms and cooked meat or chicken
    and prawns or shrimps (if used) and cook, stirring
    occasionally, for a further 10 minutes.
5   Stir in the cumin, oregano and lemon juice.

Chicken, Olives and Pineapple

Cold chicken or other poultry is mixed with sliced
stuffed olives, crushed pineapple and mayonnaise and
served on a bed of lettuce.

Serves 4

INGREDIENTS

8 oz. or more cold chicken,   pineapple
   turkey or duck   home-made mayonnaise (see
1 small jar (4 fluid oz.) stuffed   page 144–7) or good-quality
   olives   thick bought mayonnaise
1 small (13¼-oz.) can crushed   lettuce

METHOD
1   Cut the cold poultry into small dice and place in a bowl.
2   Add the sliced stuffed olives.
3   Add the drained crushed pineapple.
4   Mix together with mayonnaise and serve on a bed of
    lettuce.

Baked Chicken

Fried chicken is delicious, but the frying can smell the
house out! A crisp finish can be given to chicken without
cooking smells by baking it in the oven. Dip the washed
and dried chicken joints in well-seasoned flour, then coat
in egg and breadcrumbs. Bake for an hour at 350°F,
gas mark 4, placing the joints in a well-greased baking
dish. Pour on a basting mixture (a mixture of cooking
fat dissolved in a cupful of boiling water) from time to
time. Serve with salads and potato crisps.

Serves any number

Oven temperature: 350°F, gas mark 4

Cooking time: approximately 1 hour

INGREDIENTS

1 chicken joint per person   packet crumbs
flour for coating, well   large knob of cooking fat
   seasoned with salt and   1 cup boiling water
   pepper   salads and potato crisps
eggs

METHOD·

1 Coat the joints in well-seasoned flour by shaking the chicken and flour together in a clean plastic or strong paper bag. Shake to remove excess flour.
2 Dip in beaten egg, using a brush if necessary to coat completely.
3 Coat chicken evenly in crumbs.
4 Place on a well-greased baking dish and bake at 350°F, gas mark 4, for 1 hour. Pour on a basting mixture occasionally during baking. To make the basting mixture, pour a cupful of boiling water into a jug and add a large knob of cooking fat. When it has dissolved, stir thoroughly and use to baste a little at a time over the chicken. At the end of approximately 1 hour the chicken should be tender and the outside crisp and brown.
5 Serve with salads and potato crisps.

Chicken Waldorf

Cold chicken is mixed with cut-up celery, apple, walnuts and mayonnaise. It is served on a bed of lettuce.

Serves 4

INGREDIENTS

at least 8 oz. cold chicken or other poultry
4 sticks of celery, sliced

2 medium red-skinned eating apples, cored and diced
1½ oz. walnuts, chopped

home-made mayonnaise (see   lettuce
    pages 144–7) or good-quality   watercress and tomato for
    thick bought mayonnaise   garnish (optional)

METHOD

1   Cut the poultry into small dice.
2   Mix with the celery, apples and walnuts and fold in
    the mayonnaise.
3   Arrange lettuce leaves or shredded lettuce in the
    serving dish and pile the mixture on top. Garnish
    with watercress and tomato.

Note: If you have no left-over cold chicken, chicken
quarters can be cooked especially for this dish. If frozen
chicken is used, thaw it first and then fry in butter or oil
gently for about half an hour or until cooked through.
Drain and allow to cool. Remove meat from joints and
cut into dice or shreds.

Crunchy Chicken

This is a splendid way of re-heating cold cooked chicken.
It tastes as if you have taken the trouble to make a
luxurious sauce, but in fact its base is a condensed soup.
The chopped cooked chicken is mixed with thick condensed chicken soup (undiluted), diced celery, chopped
walnuts, chopped spring onions, lemon juice, mayonnaise,
chopped hard-boiled egg and seasoning. Cover with

crushed potato crisps and bake in a shallow heatproof dish in a hot oven for approximately 20 minutes.

Serves 3 to 4

Oven temperature: 425°F, gas mark 7

Cooking time: approximately 20 minutes

INGREDIENTS

12 oz. cooked chicken

10-oz. can condensed chicken soup (used undiluted)

4 to 5 tablespoons diced raw celery

2 oz. chopped walnuts

1 tablespoon chopped spring onions

1 tablespoon lemon juice

2 tablespoons mayonnaise

2 hard-boiled eggs, chopped

salt and pepper

1 small packet potato crisps

METHOD

1 Cut chicken into small pieces.
2 Combine in shallow heatproof dish with all the rest of the ingredients except the crisps.
3 Cover with the crushed crisps.
4 Bake at 425°F, gas mark 7, for approximately 20 minutes.

Saucy Chicken in Foil

This recipe makes a quick change from ordinary roast chicken. Add flavour and succulence to a frozen roasting chicken by cooking it with a parsley and thyme stuffing and pouring over it a sauce made from tomato ketchup, Worcestershire sauce and vinegar. Roast the whole bird wrapped in a foil parcel; this keeps in the flavour and moisture.

Serves 5–6

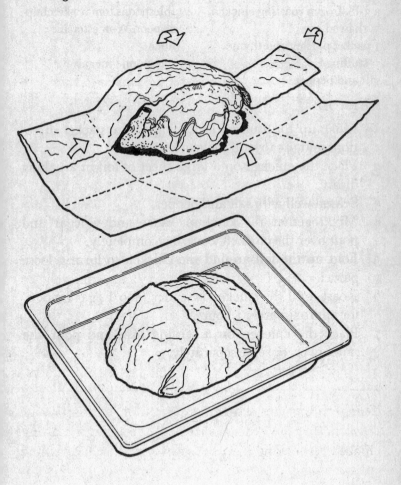

Oven temperature: 400°F, gas mark 6

Cooking time: approximately 1 hour

You will need a roll of wide kitchen foil

INGREDIENTS

a 3-lb. frozen roasting chicken, thawed

1 packet parsley and thyme stuffing

salt and pepper

4 tablespoons tomato ketchup

1 teaspoon Worcestershire sauce

1 tablespoon vinegar

METHOD

1   Make up the stuffing according to the packet directions and use to stuff the chicken.

2   Place the chicken on a large sheet of foil in a baking dish.

3   Season well with salt and pepper.

4   Mix together the ketchup, sauce and vinegar and pour over the chicken, covering completely.

5   Fold up the foil around the chicken to form a loose parcel.

6   Roast until the chicken is tender (400°F, gas mark 6, for approximately 1 hour).

7   Place the chicken on a serving dish and pour the sauce over, or serve separately.

Chapter 6
Eggs, Cheese and Flans

Cheese Scrambled Eggs

To give plenty of nourishment and flavour, add grated Cheddar cheese – 2 oz. per serving – when scrambling eggs. The grated cheese is added to the beaten raw eggs and milk and cooked gently with them.

Serves 3 (i.e. allow 2 eggs per serving)

INGREDIENTS

6 standard eggs
6 tablespoons milk
salt and pepper
6 oz. medium-strong Cheddar

cheese, grated
knob of butter
buttered toast

METHOD

1   Whisk the eggs thoroughly.
2   Whisk in the milk and seasonings.
3   Stir in the grated cheese.
4   Melt the butter over medium heat, pour in the egg

mixture and stir occasionally as for scrambled eggs, stirring more as it thickens.

5   Stop cooking the mixture when it is still slightly runny – the heat of the pan will finish the cooking.

6   Serve on or with buttered toast.

Corn Fritters

This is a rich fritter batter, made with eggs, flour, water and milk, but lightened by separating the yolks from the whites. A can of drained corn is stirred in and tablespoons of the mixture are fried in oil and butter. Serve fritters with wedges of lemon or sprinkle with Parmesan cheese. This makes a welcome supper dish for unexpected visitors.

Serves 4 or more (makes approximately 24 fritters)

INGREDIENTS

6 rounded tablespoons flour
salt
2 eggs, separated
1 tablespoon water
1 cup milk

1 can corn (drained)
lemon or grated Parmesan
   cheese
oil and knob of butter

METHOD

1   Make a well in the centre of the flour and salt, and beat in the yolks, water and some of the milk. When plopping with air, stir in the rest of the milk.

2 Leave for 30 minutes, if convenient.
3 Stiffly beat the whites of eggs and fold into the batter.
4 Stir in the drained corn.
5 Heat a heavy frying pan with oil or oil and butter for shallow-fat frying.
6 Fry tablespoons of the mixture until they are golden brown on one side. Turn and fry the other side.
7 Drain the fritters on absorbent paper and keep warm until all the mixture is used.
8 Serve with wedges of lemon or sprinkled with Parmesan cheese.

Curried Egg Mousse

The normal smoothness of an egg mousse is made more interesting by incorporating small pieces of chopped hard-boiled egg. It is flavoured subtly with mild curry.

Serves 6–8 individual dishes as a starter or 1½-pint-sized soufflé dish

INGREDIENTS

6 eggs, hard-boiled
mayonnaise (preferably home-made – see pages 144–7
1 small onion, peeled and chopped
2 teaspoons oil
1 tablespoon curry powder
1 tablespoon mango chutney

¼ pint light stock (or piece of chicken stock cube in water)
2 teaspoons gelatine
salt
pinch of cayenne pepper
⅛ pint double cream
mustard and cress or cucumber for garnish

METHOD

1   Chop eggs coarsely and mix with enough mayonnaise
    to make a fairly soft mixture.
2   Fry onion gently in oil till soft but not brown.
3   Add curry powder and stir over gentle heat for 1
    minute.
4   Add chutney and half the stock, simmer until thick.
    Sieve into the egg mixture.
5   Add gelatine to remaining stock, heat gently to dis-
    solve and add to the egg mixture.
6   Adjust seasoning.
7   Half-whip cream and fold in lightly.
8   Pour into dish, cover and chill till set.
9   Decorate with blobs of chutney and sprigs of mustard
    and cress or slices of cucumber.

Egg and Cheese Flan*

Fill a shortcrust pastry case with a layer of tomatoes, then
a savoury custard of eggs, milk, cheese and mustard.
Bake till firm and golden.

Serves 6

Oven temperature: 375°F, gas mark 5

* If frozen, warm through before eating (about 30 minutes at
  375–400°F, gas mark 5–6).

Cooking time: 40 minutes

You will need a 9-inch flan tin

INGREDIENTS

6 oz. shortcrust pastry	salt and pepper
2 eggs	$\frac{1}{4}$ pint milk
4 oz. grated Cheddar cheese	4 sliced, peeled tomatoes
1 teaspoon mustard	

METHOD

1 Line the 9-inch flan tin with the thinly rolled-out shortcrust pastry. (If you have no favourite recipe, follow that given for fork-mix pastry on a packet of Spry or Trex. You will need to use 6 oz. flour.)

2 Brush the pastry with a little of the egg white.

3 In a bowl, beat the remaining eggs and add the cheese and seasonings.

4 Heat the milk almost to boiling and pour over the egg and cheese mixture.

5 Put a layer of tomatoes on the pastry in the flan tin.

6 Pour on the egg, cheese and milk mixture.

7 Bake at 375°F, gas mark 5, for approximately 40 minutes, till firm to the touch and golden brown on top.

Green Bean Rarebit

This is a Welsh rarebit with a difference. It is made more filling and colourful by the addition of green beans and canned or dried red peppers.

Serves 4

INGREDIENTS

4 oz. sliced green beans
1 oz. butter
1 oz. flour
½ pint milk
4 oz. grated Cheddar cheese

1 red pepper, sliced (from a
    can), or 1 teaspoon dried
    peppers*
4 slices bread, toasted or
    fried

* Make sure you buy mild pimentoes, not chillies.

METHOD

1 Cook the beans, and drain. If using dried peppers
   put them to soak in boiling water for 5 minutes, then
   drain.
2 Make a white sauce by melting the butter, stirring in
   the flour and blending in the milk. Bring to the boil,
   stirring.
3 Add 3 oz. of the grated cheese.
4 Add the peppers and beans and heat through.
5 Pour the sauce over the slices of toast or fried bread.
6 Sprinkle with the remainder of the cheese and brown
   under the grill.

Hard-boiled Eggs with Lemon Sauce

This is a light summer lunch dish – hard-boiled eggs
coated with a thick white sauce, well flavoured with

lemon juice and chopped chives, or the green part of salad onions.

Serves 3

INGREDIENTS

6 hard-boiled eggs	salt and pepper
1 oz. flour	juice of $\frac{1}{2}$ lemon
1 oz. butter	fresh chives or salad onions,
$\frac{1}{2}$ pint milk	snipped small with scissors

METHOD

1 If eggs are kept in a refrigerator, remove them so that they warm to room temperature for an hour or so before plunging them in cold water, bringing them to the boil and simmering them gently for about 10 minutes as usual.

2 While the eggs are boiling, make the sauce: stir the flour and butter together over a gentle heat to make a roux (a thick paste) and continue stirring, without browning, for about 3 minutes.

3 Off the heat, gradually add the milk and stir until smooth. Return to the heat and continue stirring till it thickens. Season and continue to stir over the heat for another 3 minutes.

4 Add the lemon juice (adding more if necessary to make it taste nice and lemony).

5 Add the chives or the green part of salad onions.

6 Pour over the shelled, halved hard-boiled eggs.

Mushroom Tart

Roll out puff pastry thinly, prick and brush with egg white. Then cover with a mixture of fried sliced mushrooms and onions, seasoned and cooled and stirred with beaten egg. Bake and eat hot.

Serves 4 – or can be used for small hot canapes

Oven temperature: 400°F, gas mark 6

Cooking time: 20–30 minutes

INGREDIENTS

¾ lb. mushrooms
¼ Spanish onion or 1 small onion
oil for frying

salt and pepper
1 (7-oz.) packet puff pastry
1 large egg

METHOD

1 Slice the mushrooms thinly. Chop the onion. Fry together in oil, season and allow to cool. Drain off any surplus liquor.

2 Roll out the pastry to an oblong approximately 7 × 11 inches, the thickness of a 10p. piece. Lift onto a baking sheet. Prick. Brush with a little of the egg white.

3 Beat the egg and stir it into the mushroom and onion.

4 Spread the mixture over the pastry base.

5 Bake at 400°F, gas mark 6, for 20–30 minutes. Cut into 4 and serve hot. It can be cut into smaller pieces to use as fresh hot canapes.

Cheese and Onion Pancakes⁎

Make thin pancakes and fill them with a mixture of grated onion, grated cheese, margarine, milk, mustard, pepper and salt.

Makes 8 pancakes

INGREDIENTS

Pancakes

4 oz. plain flour
½ level teaspoon salt
1 egg
½ pint milk

Filling

1 small–medium grated onion
4 oz. grated Cheddar cheese
1 oz. margarine
4 tablespoons milk
1 rounded teaspoon mustard
salt and pepper

METHOD

1 Make the pancakes as directed in steps 1 to 7 on pages 173–4.

2 As each pancake is made, put it on a plate standing over a pan of simmering water, putting a round of greaseproof paper between each pancake and covering with the lid of a saucepan.

3 Put all the ingredients for the filling into a small saucepan and stir over gentle heat till very hot.

⁎ Pancakes may be made and frozen without fillings. Interleaf as suggested above, and separate for rapid thawing. Then use as required. They may be re-heated in a moderate oven, or over a pan of water, or as for the classic 'crêpes Suzette'.

4   Spread filling over each pancake, roll up and serve
    immediately.

Pissaladière

Around the Marseilles and Toulon area in the South of
France, Pissaladière can be bought, piping hot, by the
slice from bakeries and in the market places. It is made
from a cooked purée of onions, sometimes with tomatoes
added, spread on a base of bread dough, thinly rolled
into rounds or squares. Anchovy fillets and black olives
garnish the top. Thick slices of bread, lightly fried on one
side in oil, can be used instead of the bread dough. This
recipe has the same topping but is cooked on a quick-to-
make scone dough given to me by the Flour Advisory
Bureau. Serve Pissaladière with a green salad and a
glass of red wine.

Serves 4–6

Oven temperature: 425°F, gas mark 7

Cooking time: after about ¾-hour preparation of onion
filling, 30 minutes' baking

You will need a tin 7 × 11 × 1 inches deep

INGREDIENTS

2 lb. large onions	drained
4 tablespoons salad or olive oil	⅛ teaspoon garlic powder, or 1 clove garlic, crushed
1 (14-oz.) can tomatoes,	salt and pepper

Scone dough

12 oz. self-raising flour	about ¼ pint milk
½ level teaspoon salt	1 (2½-oz.) can anchovies and
3 oz. butter	black olives for garnish

METHOD

1 The scone dough (step 2) can be made while the onions are cooking. Slice onions and cook gently in oil in a pan with a lid. The onions should be very soft and puréed and must not brown. This takes about 40 minutes, but after 10 minutes stir in the well-drained tomatoes. A little fresh garlic or garlic powder may be added if you like. Season.

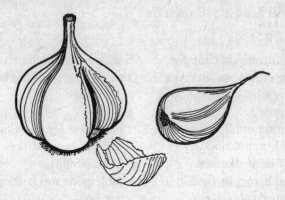

2 Meanwhile make the scone dough: Sift together flour and salt. Rub in butter until mixture resembles fine breadcrumbs. Add milk to bind to a soft dough. Roll out to a rectangle 8 × 12 inches and use to line a greased tin 7 × 11 × 1 inches deep.

3 Spread over the onion purée and arrange anchovy

fillets on top in a trellis design. Bake at 425°F, gas mark 7, for 30 minutes. Place a black olive in the centre of each trellis.

Spinach Flan*

Spinach and onion, topped with egg, cheese and cream, baked in a wholemeal pastry case and served hot.

Serves 4

Oven temperature: 400°F, gas mark 6

Cooking time: 30–40 minutes

You will need a 7–8-inch tin

INGREDIENTS

2 medium onions, chopped
2 spring onions, cut in rings
1 clove garlic, finely chopped (optional)
½ oz. butter or oil for frying
1 packet (approximately 11 oz.) frozen chopped spinach, or 3 lb. fresh chopped spinach
salt

6 oz. wholemeal flour
1 oz. butter, or 1 fluid oz. oil, for dough
2 eggs
1 oz. cheese (grated Cheddar, grated Parmesan or Mozzarella)
1 tablespoon top milk or cream

❉ If freezing, either partially bake the case 'blind' first, or brush base of pastry with white of egg or oil before adding filling, to prevent it soaking into the pastry. Bake, cool, freeze. Thaw and re-heat in one operation (about 40 minutes at 300°F, gas mark 2).

METHOD

1   Brown the onions, spring onions and garlic in the butter, then stir in the spinach till softened, adding salt to taste. Simmer for one minute longer and put to one side.

2   Place the wholemeal flour in a bowl and rub in the butter or oil. Add a pinch of salt and work in enough water to make a firm dough. Knead well and roll out ¼-inch thick to line a shallow greased 7–8-inch tin (or, if you wish, press into the tin without rolling).

3   Fill the pastry case with the drained spinach mixture.

4   Beat the eggs, add the cheese and cream and pour this mixture on top of the spinach.

5   Bake at 400°F, gas mark 6, for 30 to 40 minutes. Serve hot.

Stuffed Baked Omelettes

This is how to turn an omelette into a satisfying, filling meal. Stuff the omelettes with ratatouille, coat with a cheese sauce and heat in the oven. It is not necessary to make ratatouille especially for this dish; to save time, make more ratatouille than you need (see page 121) one day and use up the rest for this recipe later, or use frozen ratatouille.

Serves 3 or more according to the number of omelettes made

Oven temperature: 400°F, gas mark 6
Baking time: 10 minutes

INGREDIENTS

2 or 3 tablespoons ratatouille (see page 121) for each omelette
3 or more omelettes (each with two eggs)
½ pint cheese sauce:

1 oz. butter	½ pint milk
1 oz. flour	3 oz. grated Cheddar cheese

METHOD

1   Make individual omelettes (see next recipe) in a
    small pan, stuffing each one with ratatouille and
    putting into an ovenproof dish until all are ready.

2   Make the cheese sauce to a coating consistency and
    pour it right over the stuffed omelettes.

3   Bake for about 10 minutes at 400°F, gas mark 6, till
    bubbling hot.

4   Carefully lift each omelette with stuffing and sauce
    onto a heated plate.

Individual Omelettes

INGREDIENTS

2 eggs	2 tablespoons cold water
salt and pepper	½ oz. butter

METHOD

1   Beat eggs lightly with seasoning. Stir in water.

2   Pour eggs into sizzling butter in a small frying pan.

3 Draw cooked eggs from edge of pan inwards and with a palette knife raise edge and tilt pan to allow raw eggs to run through to cook on pan base.
4 While top is still runny, fold omelette and turn out.

Chapter 7
Vegetables

Brussels Sprouts (or Cabbage) Mornay

To make a change from cauliflower cheese, serve lightly boiled brussels sprouts or shredded cabbage coated with a cheese sauce, sprinkled with grated cheese and bread-crumbs and browned under the grill.

Serves 3 or 4

INGREDIENTS

1 lb. small fresh or frozen brussels sprouts, or 1 small cabbage, shredded

1½ oz. butter
1½ oz. flour } white sauce
¾ pint milk

4 oz. Cheddar cheese, grated
pepper, salt and mustard
1 oz. golden breadcrumbs

METHOD

1   Boil the vegetables in lightly salted water till just

tender. Place the chosen vegetables in a 1-pint oven-
proof serving dish.

2   Meanwhile make the white sauce (page 99) and add
3 oz. of the cheese. Season to taste.

3   Pour the sauce over the sprouts or cabbage.

4   Sprinkle with breadcrumbs and the remaining cheese.

5   Grill quickly till golden brown.

Buttery Cabbage

Boil shredded cabbage till just tender, drain it, then toss
it in butter, brown sugar and a little vinegar. Stew a
further 5 minutes. This gives a buttery cabbage, with the
merest hint of sugar and vinegar.

Number of servings according to size of cabbage

INGREDIENTS

1 small well-hearted cabbage   1 teaspoon brown sugar
large knob of butter or   salt and pepper
    margarine   1 small teaspoon vinegar

METHOD

1   Cut the cabbage in 4, shred it medium-fine and wash
in a colander.

2   Boil in 1 inch of salted boiling water with the lid
tightly on the pan for approximately 5 minutes, till
tender but still slightly firm. Drain.

3   Put a large knob of butter or margarine in the pan,
add the drained cabbage and the sugar, seasoning

and vinegar (only a small amount of vinegar is used because its flavour must not predominate).

4   Stir, replace the lid and stew gently for a further 5 minutes.
5   Serve with the buttery juice.

Caraway Cabbage

Add a few caraway seeds to the water when cooking cabbage – the flavours marry perfectly.

Serves 4–6, depending on size of cabbage

INGREDIENTS

1 cabbage   knob of butter
2 teaspoons caraway seeds

METHOD

1   Shred the cabbage and wash it thoroughly in a colander.
2   Boil 1 inch salted water in a saucepan with a tightly fitting lid.
3   When the water is boiling rapidly, add the cabbage and the caraway seeds.
4   Boil till just tender – about 5–7 minutes.
5   Drain carefully so that you do not pour away too many of the caraway seeds.
6   Serve immediately with a knob of butter melting into the cabbage.

Creamed Vegetables

Cook a mixture of sliced vegetables in salted water. Drain, reserving the liquor to mix with milk. Make a pouring sauce with the vegetable water and milk and a roux of flour and butter. Re-heat the vegetables in the sauce, season and garnish with chopped parsley.

Serves 4

INGREDIENTS

3–4 cups of vegetables, e.g.	water
sliced peeled carrots	milk
sliced peeled potatoes	1½ oz. butter
sliced leeks	1½ oz. flour
sliced celery	pepper
salt	1 tablespoon chopped parsley

METHOD

1 Simmer the vegetables together in lightly salted water till tender.
2 Drain through a sieve into a measuring jug.
3 Use sufficient vegetable water, mixed with milk, to make 1 pint.
4 In the saucepan stir together the butter and flour to make a roux. Stir over the heat for 3 minutes.
5 Gradually add the milk and vegetable stock, stirring till smooth and heating to make a sauce.
6 Re-heat the vegetables in this sauce. Season with pepper and more salt if necessary.
7 Sprinkle with chopped parsley.

Note: If you have had to buy more vegetables than you need for 4 cups of sliced vegetables (e.g. a whole head of celery when you only need a few stalks) cut up the remaining raw vegetables to make a soup.

Grated Potato Pancakes

Grated potato is mixed with beaten egg and seasoning and either onion salt or grated onion. Large teaspoons of the mixture are fried in hot oil, flattening as you fry. Turn when golden brown.

Serves any number

INGREDIENTS

1 large potato per person   onion salt or grated onion
1 standard egg per person   frying oil
salt and pepper

METHOD

1   Peel the potatoes and grate coarsely. Drain off moisture.
2   Beat the eggs and add to the potatoes with the seasonings and onion salt or a little grated onion. Stir well.
3   Heat oil in a large frying pan (enough oil for shallow-fat frying) and when very hot drop in large teaspoons

of the mixture, well apart so that you can flatten them.

4 When golden brown, turn and fry the other side. Allow plenty of time for frying.

5 Drain on absorbent paper and serve very hot.

Kale and Lemon

Curly kale is a strong, dark green vegetable, rich in vitamins A and C. Shred it roughly like greens, boil in the minimum of water, drain well and serve thoroughly sprinkled with the juice of a lemon.

Serves 4

INGREDIENTS

1 lb. curly kale   1 lemon, squeezed
salt

METHOD

1 Wash the kale, remove the coarsest of the stems and roughly tear the kale as you do for spring greens.

2 Pour about 1 inch of boiling salted water into a saucepan, add the kale and boil for about 10 minutes with the lid tightly on the pan.

3 Drain thoroughly.

4 Put into the vegetable dish and pour over the juice of a whole lemon. Serve immediately.

Leeks and Greens

This is for those who like vegetables tender but still crisp, cut into strips and cooked in the shortest possible time. The cooking liquor is a couple of tablespoons each of water and margarine, flavoured with a little sugar. The ½-inch strips of vegetables are simmered for the minimum time – for these, approximately 7–10 minutes – before they are served with the small amount of cooking liquor.

Serves 4 or 5

INGREDIENTS

1 lb. leeks
1 lb. spring greens, spring cabbage or Savoy
2 tablespoons water

2 tablespoons margarine
1 teaspoon sugar
salt and pepper

METHOD

1   Remove coarse outer leaves, tops and roots from the leeks. Wash the leeks, cut lengthwise in half, and rinse very thoroughly under the tap to remove all hidden grit. Cut in ½–1-inch lengths.

2   Wash the greens, cut in quarters and cut these also in ½–1-inch lengths.

3   Put the water, margarine and sugar in a saucepan over moderate heat; when the fat has melted add the vegetables. Place the lid tightly on the pan.

4   Simmer the vegetables gently until just cooked, approximately 7–10 minutes. Season with salt and pepper and serve immediately with the cooking liquor.

Mushrooms, Quick-Grilled

Grill in butter for 4 minutes, turning once. By this quick-grilling method, the outsides of the mushrooms become brown and the insides are still beautifully soft and juicy, with no loss of size and shape. Serve on toast or as an accompaniment to a meat or fish dish.

Serves 3–4

INGREDIENTS

½ lb. mushrooms – semi-open caps
butter

little lemon juice
salt and pepper
toast (optional)

METHOD

1   Trim the stalks of each mushroom to the level of the cap. Wash and shake fairly dry.
2   Make toast.
3   Melt plenty of butter in the grill pan, and when it is hot dip the mushrooms in it and grill, skin-side up-wards, under strong heat *for 2 minutes only*. The stalks, dipped in the butter, can be grilled at the same time.
4   Turn the mushrooms over and put a squeeze of lemon juice and a pinch of salt and pepper on the gills. Turn the stalks at the same time.
5   Grill *for a further 2 minutes*, again under a strong heat.

Parsnips in Cider

The basic idea is to produce browned, slightly caramel-ized parsnips with a small amount of fluid in the dish. Parboil the sliced parsnips, toss them in butter and brown sugar, add cider and bake in a flat, open heatproof dish.

Serves 4

Oven temperature: 400°F, gas mark 6
Cooking time: 30–40 minutes

INGREDIENTS

4 medium parsnips   salt and black pepper
2 tablespoons soft brown sugar   scant ¼ pint cider
1–2 oz. butter

METHOD

1 Peel the parsnips and slice about 1 inch thick.
2 Boil in salted water till almost tender. Drain.
3 Melt the butter and sugar in a flattish open oven-proof dish, and stir the parsnips around.
4 Sprinkle with salt and black pepper.
5 Pour on the cider.
6 Brown in a hot oven, 400°F, gas mark 6, for about 30 to 40 minutes, topping up the cider if too much evaporates.

Peas, French Fashion

We are so used to cooking frozen peas in a few minutes that it makes a flavour change, in season, to buy fresh peas and stew them for half an hour with butter, sugar, seasoning, small onions, lettuce and the minimum of water.

Serves 3 or 4

You will need a saucepan with a tight-fitting lid

INGREDIENTS

knob of butter
2 small onions, quartered, or
   6 pickling onions
1 tablespoon warm water
1 lump of sugar

1 small round lettuce,
   quartered and well washed
1 lb. peas, after shelling
salt and pepper

METHOD

1 Melt the butter and toss the onions in it for a few minutes, without browning.
2 Add the water and sugar.
3 Lift the 4 pieces of lettuce, dripping wet, into the pan.
4 Add the shelled peas and season lightly.
5 Put the lid on the pan and heat very gently, shaking occasionally to prevent burning. The peas should be tender in half an hour. Serve with the onions and lettuce and the buttery liquid poured over.

Peas with Hot Bacon Dressing

Frozen peas have become so popular with the British family that you should sometimes give them a new lease of life by tossing the cooked peas in a mixture of hot melted butter and demerara sugar, flavoured with fried chopped bacon.

Serves 4 to 6

INGREDIENTS

1 lb. frozen petits pois	chopped finely
2 oz. butter	1 tablespoon demerara sugar
3 rashers streaky bacon,	salt and pepper

METHOD

1 Cook the peas according to pack instructions and drain.
2 Melt the butter in the empty pan, add the demerara sugar and stir until the sugar has dissolved.
3 Add the chopped bacon and cook gently for 3 minutes.
4 Toss in the peas to re-heat.
5 Check the seasoning before serving.

Potatoes Baked in their Jackets

One of our favourite ways of serving main-crop potatoes is baked in their jackets. They either need plenty of salted butter mashed inside once they are cooked and halved on the plate; or for a change mash in a small individual portion of Boursin cheese (the type flavoured with garlic and herbs). Eat the well-scrubbed skin – it's the best part.

Serves any number

Oven temperature: 375–400°F, gas mark 5–6

Cooking time: $\frac{3}{4}$–1 hour

INGREDIENTS

1 (6-oz.) potato per person
butter

small Boursin cheeses with garlic and herbs (optional)

METHOD

1   Scrub the potatoes well and dry with kitchen paper.
2   Prick all over the skin with a fork, to prevent bursting in the oven.
3   Rub the skin with butter (use the outer wrapper from a packet of butter to avoid messy fingers).
4   Bake at 375–400°F, gas mark 5–6, for $\frac{3}{4}$ to 1 hour. You can buy a holder, consisting of metal prongs, on which to impale the raw potatoes. This holds them firmly and the metal conducts the heat right through to the centre, so that they cook evenly and a little more quickly. They are done when they 'give' when pressed with thumb and fingers.
5   Cut in half and mash in plenty of salted butter or the Boursin cheese.

Roast Potatoes

If potatoes are roasted round the joint they are inclined to be greasy. They are crisp and a pleasing golden colour if instead they are roasted in a separate pan in margarine and oil. Some people use chicken fat instead of margarine and oil.

Serves 4 to 6

Oven temperature: 375–400°F, gas mark 5–6

Cooking time: $\frac{3}{4}$–1 hour

INGREDIENTS

2 lb. potatoes
$\frac{1}{4}$ lb. margarine ⎫
1 tablespoon   ⎬ or chicken fat
  cooking oil ⎭
salt

METHOD

1 Peel the potatoes thinly and cut in halves or quarters to make small portions. A very large potato may even need to be cut into 6.
2 Put the margarine and oil in a roasting tin in the oven to melt, at 375–400°F, gas mark 5–6 (or use chicken fat).
3 Parboil the potatoes, i.e. boil for about 3 minutes so that they just begin to soften on the outside.
4 Drain and transfer to the hot fat, salting well and turning them in the pan.

5   Roast in the hottest part of the oven until they are
    tender and crisp and golden brown on the outside.
    They are best turned once during the roasting.

Ratatouille*

Stew slowly in oil a mixture of onions, aubergines, courgettes, peppers and tomatoes. Season with salt, pepper
and powdered garlic and sprinkle liberally with chopped
parsley.

Serves 4

You need a saucepan or frying pan with a lid

INGREDIENTS

olive oil
2 medium onions
1 large aubergine
2 courgettes
2 large sweet peppers

1 large can peeled tomatoes
salt, pepper and powdered
   garlic
parsley (optional)

METHOD

1   Chop the onions and sauté slowly in olive oil in a
    saucepan or frying pan. The oil should be just enough
    to cover the bottom of the pan.
2   Cut the unpeeled aubergine in cubes and add to the
    onions.
3   Slice the courgettes and add to the pan.
4   Remove the pips and stalks from the peppers and

❋ Suitable for freezing.

dice the peppers small. Add to the pan. Stir all together.

5   Add the peeled tomatoes with their juice.
6   Put a lid on the pan and stew slowly for about ¾ hour.
7   Season to taste and sprinkle, if desired, with chopped
    parsley.

Red (or White) Cabbage, Sweet and Sour

Use either red or white cabbage. Shred it, add a sliced
cooking apple and simmer with a knob of butter and a
little water. When tender, thicken with a mixture of
flour, brown sugar and vinegar.

Serves 6

INGREDIENTS

1 medium-sized red or white   salt and pepper
  cabbage   2 tablespoons flour
1 large cooking apple   4 tablespoons demerara sugar
knob of butter   2 tablespoons vinegar

METHOD

1   Trim the cabbage, shred and wash.
2   Peel, core and slice the apple fairly thinly.
3   Melt the butter in a saucepan and stir in the cabbage
    and apple.
4   Season with a little salt and pepper.

5   Pour on about an inch of boiling water. Cover the
    pan and boil till the cabbage is just tender.
6   Stir together the flour, sugar and vinegar.
7   Pour onto this mixture some of the vegetable water
    and mix till smooth. Return it to the pan and stir
    over the heat for a few minutes before serving.

Runner Beans, Italian Style (1)*

If you tire of plain boiled runner beans, try flavouring
them the Italian way; first fry the cut-up beans for a few
moments in a little olive oil, season, then add peeled
tomatoes and stew with the lid on the saucepan for about
40 minutes.

Serves 4 or 5

INGREDIENTS

1 lb. runner beans   15-oz. can peeled tomatoes
olive oil   (or 1 lb. fresh tomatoes)
salt and pepper

METHOD

1   String the beans, wash and slice across in small
    pieces (this is quicker than slicing them lengthwise).
2   Just cover the bottom of a medium-sized saucepan
    with a little olive oil, heat, and fry the beans rapidly
    in it for a minute or two.

* Suitable for freezing.

3   Add salt and pepper.
4   Drain a can of peeled tomatoes free from juice and
     add the tomatoes to the pan. (Alternatively, peel
     fresh tomatoes by dipping them for a few minutes in
     boiling water, cooling in cold water, and slipping the
     skins off. Add the cut-up fresh tomatoes to the beans.)
5   Put the lid on the pan and simmer gently for 40
     minutes. Serve with the juices from the pan.

Runner Beans, Italian Style (2)

For an alternative recipe using frozen beans, try the
following. You will need a large frying pan with a lid or
a saucepan with a lid.

INGREDIENTS

$1\frac{1}{2}$ oz. butter   freshly ground black pepper
1 lb. frozen sliced green beans   salt
1 ($7\frac{1}{2}$-oz.) can tomatoes   1 oz. Cheddar cheese, grated
$\frac{1}{2}$ teaspoon marjoram   1 oz. crisp breadcrumbs
$\frac{1}{2}$ teaspoon Worcestershire
  sauce

METHOD

1   Melt the butter and fry the beans lightly for 2
     minutes.
2   Add the contents of the can of tomatoes, marjoram,
     Worcestershire sauce and seasonings.

3 Bring to the boil and simmer for 5 minutes, with the
   lid on.
4 Serve in a vegetable dish with the cheese and breadcrumbs sprinkled on top.

Creamed Spinach

To make spinach go further use this method. Boil fresh
leaf spinach in the usual way and drain off the cooking
liquor into a basin. Make a thick white sauce, using the
spinach liquor instead of milk. Roughly chop up the
spinach and then you can bring back its bulk by stirring
it till boiling with the well-seasoned spinach sauce.

Serves 3

INGREDIENTS

1 lb. fresh leaf spinach $\frac{1}{2}$ pint liquor from the spinach
1 oz. flour   salt, pepper and nutmeg
1 oz. butter

METHOD

1 Trim the stalks and wash the spinach well in several
   waters till no grit remains.
2 Lift the dripping wet spinach into a large saucepan
   without adding any more water.
3 Bring to the boil on slow–medium heat, with the lid
   tightly on the pan. Stir occasionally. After 5 or 10

minutes the spinach will be softened (test with a knife) and the liquor will have come out of it.

4 Stand a colander in a bowl. Empty the entire con-

tents of the pan into the colander, pressing the spinach down lightly to drain.

5   Using the edge of an old saucer, chop the spinach roughly – it is easier to use the saucer than a knife.

6   Melt the butter in a small pan, add the flour and stir over medium heat to make a roux (a thick paste of butter and flour). Stir over the heat for about 3 minutes.

7   Measure ½ pint of liquor from the spinach and add gradually to the roux, stirring well to make it smooth. Bring to the boil.

8   Season with salt, pepper and a good pinch of nutmeg. Boil for a minute or two.

9   Return the spinach to the large spinach pan. Add the sauce, mix well and re-heat thoroughly before serving.

Swede and Carrots

Boil cut-up peeled swede and carrots together. When thoroughly cooked, drain and mash well and season with salt and freshly ground black pepper. Top with a knob of butter.

Serves 4

INGREDIENTS

1 large swede
1 lb. carrots
salt

freshly ground black pepper
knob of butter

METHOD

1 Peel the swede thickly, wash and cut up.
2 Peel the carrots thinly and if necessary cut in half.
3 Boil together in salted water until thoroughly cooked – this may take 20 to 30 minutes. Test for tenderness with a sharp knife.
4 Drain thoroughly.
5 Mash with a potato masher, or use the end of a rolling pin to smash the vegetables together.
6 Taste for seasoning and serve with a knob of butter.

Stuffed Peppers

Before you start, cook the rice, hard-boil the eggs and grate the cheese. The peppers are stuffed with a mixture of rice, onions, garlic, hard-boiled eggs and cheese, flavoured with parsley, oregano and sesame seeds. Fresh stewed tomatoes are poured around when they have almost finished baking.

Serves 4

Oven temperature: 375°F, gas mark 5

Cooking time: approximately 1 hour (may be longer if the peppers are very firm)

INGREDIENTS

4 large peppers
olive oil
2 tablespoons butter

1 small onion, finely chopped
1 clove garlic, crushed
1 cup cooked rice

½ teaspoon parsley, chopped
½ teaspoon oregano
salt and pepper
2 hard-boiled eggs, chopped
2 tablespoons grated
  Parmesan cheese

2 oz. Mozzarella or fresh soft
  cheese
sesame seeds (optional)
4 ripe tomatoes, peeled and
  chopped

METHOD

1 Remove the stalks and seeds without breaking the peppers. Slice the tops off the peppers and reserve to use as lids.

2 In a frying pan sauté the onion and garlic in the olive oil and butter, and when translucent add the cooked rice, parsley and oregano. Continue cooking for a further 5 minutes, mixing well and seasoning to taste.

3 Take the rice mixture from the heat and add the eggs and cheese (the heat will mix in the soft Mozzarella).

4 Place peppers in a baking dish and spoon in the mixture. Sprinkle the tops with sesame seeds if desired.

5 Put on the lids. Pour in a little water and bake at 375°F, gas mark 5, for 40 minutes.

6 Heat the tomatoes in a pan with a little garlic (optional), season, pour over the peppers and bake for 15 minutes or longer until the peppers are soft.

Vegetarian Rice

Brown rice, like other rice, can be cooked in quantity and kept for several days in the refrigerator until wanted. This dish uses two cups of brown rice, which are cooked and fried with onions, garlic, carrots, celery, mushrooms, dried walnuts, raisins, cabbage and bean sprouts. It is further flavoured with parsley, cinnamon and salt and pepper. Serve with tahini (ground sesame seed paste) or with Chinese egg slices (beaten egg fried in a flat pan and then slashed into strips – see next recipe).

Serves 5 or 6

INGREDIENTS

2 cups brown rice
4–6 tablespoons oil
2 large onions, chopped
1 clove garlic, chopped
2 small carrots, thinly sliced
1 stalk celery, chopped
2 oz. mushrooms, sliced
1 doz. walnuts, chopped
    coarsely

2 oz. raisins
1 teaspoon chopped parsley
$\frac{1}{4}$ teaspoon cinnamon
salt and pepper
$\frac{1}{2}$ small cabbage, finely sliced
2 oz. bean sprouts
tamari or soy sauce

METHOD

1   Boil the rice in plenty of salted water.
2   Heat the oil in a large heavy pan. Gently brown the onions, garlic, carrots and celery. Cook for 10 minutes over reduced heat.
3   Add the mushrooms, walnuts, raisins, parsley, cinnamon and seasonings and cook a further 10 minutes.
4   Add the cabbage with a little more oil if necessary, cooking until it is heated and turning it constantly.
5   Add the rice and bean sprouts, mix them well, and cook for a further 5 minutes. (Add a little water if it sticks.)
6   Tamari (or soy sauce) may be added during the cooking process or served once cooked.

7   Serve with tahini or Chinese egg slices (see next recipe).

Chinese Egg Slices

INGREDIENTS

4 eggs   chopped parsley
1 tablespoon top milk   knob of butter
salt and pepper

METHOD

1   Beat the eggs with the top milk, seasonings and parsley.
2   Melt butter in a large flat frying pan and fry the egg mixture.
3   When cooked, slash into thin slices with a knife.
4   Serve on top of Vegetarian Rice (above).

Chapter 8
Salads

Avocado Salad

I first saw this salad dressing in Israel. I was intrigued by the hard-boiled egg mashed into it and the tangy flavour of the wine vinegar and lemon juice mixed with olive oil, mustard and plenty of sugar. In this salad, the dressing is poured over lettuce hearts, cut-up avocado, orange and tomato.

Serves 4

INGREDIENTS

1 large lettuce
1 large ripe avocado
1 large orange
4 tomatoes
1 clove garlic
1 tablespoon wine vinegar
2 tablespoons lemon juice
4 tablespoons olive oil
½ teaspoon mustard
1 tablespoon sugar
1 hard-boiled egg, mashed
salt and pepper

METHOD

1   Rub a salad bowl with the cut garlic.

2   Wash the lettuce leaves and shake dry. Shred or tear
     into pieces. Peel and cube the avocado. Peel and
     slice the orange and cut into wedges. Quarter the
     tomatoes.
3   Place the lettuce, avocado, orange and tomatoes in
     the bowl.
4   With a spoon, mix the vinegar, lemon juice, oil,
     mustard, sugar, egg, salt and pepper in a basin, or
     shake them together in a screw-top jar.
5   Pour over the salad. Toss with two spoons and serve
     immediately.

Cottage Cheese Salad

Serves 3 or 4

INGREDIENTS

Dressing
3 tablespoons tarragon
   vinegar
2 tablespoons olive oil
1 tablespoon parsley, finely
   chopped
small clove garlic, crushed
freshly ground black pepper

shake of paprika
saltspoon of salt
Salad
cos lettuce leaves
spring onions, finely sliced
tomatoes in wedges
½ cucumber, sliced
large carton cottage cheese

METHOD

1   Mix all the ingredients for the dressing together.
2   Mix the salad. Place the cottage cheese on top.

3   Remove the garlic and pour the dressing over the
    mixed salad and cottage cheese.

Cucumber Salad, Scandinavian Style

Marinade wafer-thin slices of fresh cucumber for a few
hours in vinegar diluted with water, seasoned and
sweetened with plenty of sugar.

Serve very cold.

INGREDIENTS

1 cucumber, unpeeled
4 tablespoons malt vinegar
2 tablespoons water
4 teaspoons granulated or
   caster sugar

$\frac{1}{4}$ teaspoon salt
good shake of pepper
pinch of mustard

METHOD

1   In the serving bowl mix the vinegar, water, sugar and
    seasonings.
2   Wash the cucumber and cut it into wafer-thin slices.
    Use an electric slicer, the fine slicer of a Mouli, a
    mandoline slicer or just a very sharp knife – the
    slices need to be as thin as a potato crisp.
3   Marinade the cucumber in the vinegar solution for
    an hour or more, putting it in a refrigerator for
    preference.

Cucumber and Orange Salad

This makes half a cucumber go a long way and there is
no need to peel it unless you want to. Slice the cucumber
and pieces of orange (cut free from pith) into an oil and
vinegar or French dressing.

Serves 4

INGREDIENTS

½ cucumber

1 large orange

3 tablespoons wine vinegar

3 tablespoons salad oil

1 teaspoon sugar

½ teaspoon salt

shake of pepper

pinch of mustard

METHOD

1   Pour the oil and vinegar into a bottle (use an old oil
    or vinegar bottle which has a cap, or a screw-top jar).
    As they do not mix, you can tell when there are equal
    quantities and it does not matter if there are not
    exactly 3 tablespoons of each – some people like a
    little more oil than vinegar.

2   With the aid of a pointed funnel made out of paper,
    add the sugar and seasonings.

3   Slice the cucumber very thinly into the salad bowl.

4   Peel the orange round and round with a sharp knife,
    removing the pith as well as the peel. Slice and cut
    the orange into small pieces and add to the cucumber.

5   Put the cap on the bottle of dressing and shake it
    vigorously to mix it before pouring it over the salad.

Note: Although a small recipe is given for this oil and vinegar dressing it is a good idea to make a bottleful at a time. For large amounts you may like to add a little more oil than vinegar; taste for flavouring when adding the sugar and seasonings. With a bottleful, all you need to do when a recipe calls for an oil and vinegar dressing is to give the bottle a good shake and you have the dressing ready for use.

Mushroom and Orange Salad

As an alternative to the above, slice very thinly $\frac{1}{4}$ lb. raw button mushrooms and add the flesh of 2 oranges. Mix as above with the oil and vinegar dressing.

Green or Red Salad

Make a mixture of cubed unpeeled cucumber and unpeeled apple, sliced celery and chopped pepper. Dress with a mixture of mayonnaise and French dressing. This salad can either be all green, or can be green and red if you use a red-skinned apple and a red pepper.

Serves 4

INGREDIENTS

½ cucumber   1 tablespoon mayonnaise
1 apple   1 tablespoon French dressing
2 sticks celery   (see page 137)
1 green or red pepper

METHOD

1   Wash all the vegetables and the apple.
2   If for colour you would like to keep the peel on each
    piece of cucumber, cut it lengthwise into 6 or 8 and
    then across into small pieces.
3   Core and cube the unpeeled apple.
4   Slice the celery.
5   Discard the pips and stalk from the pepper. Cut the
    pepper into slices and then into small pieces.
6   Toss in a salad bowl with the mayonnaise and
    French dressing.

Hawaiian Salad

This is an unusual pasta salad, flavoured with mixed
vegetables, crushed pineapple and currants. It is served
cold, tossed in a French dressing and garnished with
chopped parsley.

Serves 4 as a main salad in place of potatoes

INGREDIENTS

3 oz. pasta shells
5-oz. pack frozen mixed
   vegetables
1 tablespoon
   vinegar
2 tablespoons   } French
   olive oil   } dressing
salt and
   pepper

3 oz. crushed pineapple,
   drained
1 tablespoon currants
parsley, chopped

METHOD

1 Cook the pasta shells and the mixed vegetables
   according to pack instructions.
2 Drain, place in a sieve and run them under cold
   water. Allow to cool.
3 Stir the French dressing ingredients thoroughly together. (It is quicker to mix them by shaking them
   together in a screw-top jar or bottle.)
4 Toss all the ingredients in the dressing and serve
   garnished with parsley.

Orange Coleslaw

Give interest to a plain coleslaw of cabbage and carrot
with the addition of thinly sliced onion (optional) and
chopped green pepper and oranges. Bind together with
home-made mayonnaise (see pages 144–7) or a good

bought mayonnaise and a little additional white wine vinegar if necessary.

Serves 6 to 8

INGREDIENTS

1 lb. white salad cabbage, shredded

1 mild onion, peeled and thinly sliced (optional)

2 carrots, peeled and coarsely grated

1 green pepper, cored and chopped

3 oranges

mayonnaise (see pages 144–7)

white wine vinegar

METHOD

1 Mix together the prepared vegetables.

2 Peel the oranges free from pith, slice and cut into small pieces. Add to the vegetables.

3 Just before serving toss with mayonnaise, adding a little extra wine vinegar to taste.

Potato Salad Tartare

Start with a potato salad but mix with the mayonnaise some chopped capers, pickled cucumbers and parsley. Excellent served with fish.

Serves 4

INGREDIENTS

2 lb. new potatoes

½ pint mayonnaise, preferably home-made (see pages 144–7)

1–2 tablespoons roughly chopped capers

2 tablespoons finely chopped   2 tablespoons roughly
   pickled cucumbers   chopped parsley

METHOD

1 Scrape the potatoes, cutting the larger ones in half to
   match the smaller ones in size if necessary.
2 Boil till just tender (test by piercing with a sharp
   knife).
3 Meanwhile mix the rest of the ingredients in a serving
   bowl.
4 Cut the cooked potatoes into small cubes and while
   still warm stir them into the mayonnaise mixture.
5 Allow to get quite cold before serving.

Rice Salad*

Add chopped-up celery, green pepper, tomatoes, dried
walnuts and sultanas to cold cooked rice.

Serves 4

INGREDIENTS

1 cup long-grain rice   2 tomatoes, skinned
2½ cups water   1 tablespoon walnuts
1 teaspoon salt   1 tablespoon sultanas, washed
2 or 3 sticks celery   French dressing (optional)
½ green pepper   (see page 137)

* Frozen cooked rice could be used for this – thawed first, of
   course.

METHOD

1 Cook the rice according to packet directions (generally these are: bring 1 cup washed rice to the boil in
   2½ cups water with 1 teaspoon salt, stir and cook
   covered over a low heat for about 15 minutes or until
   tender).
2 Chop up the celery, pepper, tomatoes and walnuts
   and mix with the sultanas into the cooked rice. If
   possible, put in the refrigerator to get quite cold.
3 To give extra flavour and moisture, stir in a few
   tablespoons of French dressing (see page 137) before
   serving.

Chapter 9
Stuffings, Sauces, Gravies and Accompaniments

Herb, Almond and Raisin Stuffing*

(for turkey or chicken)

At Christmas I make a special parsley stuffing for the turkey by adding to the usual herb forcemeat stuffing some raisins and chopped almonds. If there is any red wine open I use that to bind the stuffing, or otherwise use milk or stock. The raw liver of the bird can be chopped into the stuffing if you wish. In fact, this is so good that I now use the quantities below to stuff roast chicken at other times of the year.

Quantity: sufficient for an average-size roasting chicken.

Double the quantities for stuffing the neck end of a turkey

✳ May be frozen for up to a month before required. It is wiser not to stuff birds before freezing as they may be stored for longer than any stuffings.

INGREDIENTS

2 oz. bacon
4 oz. fresh white breadcrumbs
1 oz. shredded suet
½ tablespoon mixed dried
  herbs
1 tablespoon parsley, chopped
grated rind of ½ lemon

1 oz. blanched almonds,
  coarsely chopped
1 oz. seedless raisins
chopped raw turkey or chicken
  liver (optional)
1 standard egg, beaten
salt and pepper
milk, stock or red wine to bind

METHOD

1 Cut the bacon into small pieces with scissors or a
   sharp knife and fry in its own fat without browning.
   Drain.

2 Mix the bacon with the rest of the ingredients, using
   just enough milk, stock or red wine to bind the mixture together.

Mayonnaise, 4-Minute Method

Mayonnaise is often regarded as temperamental or just
plain difficult to make without an electric mixer or
liquidizer. This is not so. Mayonnaise can be stirred by
hand in only 4 minutes if you:

1 Use a metal tablespoon to stir it.
2 Use a 1½-pint bowl to make ½ pint mayonnaise.
3 Make sure that all the white has drained from the
   egg yolks.

4 Use oil and egg yolks at room temperature.

5 First pour on the oil in teaspoons (it is not necessary to add it drop by drop). As soon as the mixture thickens, quicken the process.

If you take the above simple measures, the mixture should not curdle, but if it does, beat the curdled mixture into another egg yolk.

Yield: approximately ½ pint mayonnaise.

INGREDIENTS

2 egg yolks (from large or standard-weight eggs)
½ pint olive or corn oil
½ teaspoon salt
¼ teaspoon dry mustard
freshly ground black pepper

about 2 dessertspoons vinegar or lemon juice (use tarragon, white wine or cider vinegar)
cream (optional)

METHOD

1 Place yolks, seasonings and 1 dessertspoon of the vinegar or lemon juice into a 1½-pint basin. Whisk well together with a fork.

2 Change to a metal tablespoon and start stirring. Slowly add the oil. It is unnecessary to add it drop by drop – approximate teaspoonsful will work and help to do the job quickly.

3 As the mixture begins to thicken, the oil can be added more quickly. Keep on stirring. (It helps to keep the bowl steady if you stand it on a damp plastic or fabric dish cloth.) It should only take about 4 minutes to blend in all the oil.

4 Adjust seasonings and vinegar to taste. If you like,

you can thin it down and make it go further with a
little cream just before serving.

5   It is best kept in a covered jar in the refrigerator. It
is an uncooked sauce, so will not keep indefinitely.

Mayonnaise with Liquidizer

If you have a liquidizer or blender, you can make
mayonnaise in a matter of seconds.

INGREDIENTS

2 large eggs (use whites as   2 rounded teaspoons sugar
  well as yolks)   1 flat teaspoon mustard
4 tablespoons vinegar or lemon   shake of pepper
  juice   about ¾ pint oil
2 flat teaspoons salt

METHOD

1   Break the eggs into the liquidizer.
2   Add the vinegar or lemon juice and the seasonings.
3   Put the lid on the liquidizer and switch to slowest
    speed.
4   Remove lid, or cap from centre of lid, and pour the
    oil in a thin trickle until the mayonnaise thickens and
    can take no more oil.
5   Switch to high to absorb the last drops of oil.
6   Store covered in the refrigerator.

Note: To prevent curdling, all the ingredients are best
used at room temperature. If the mayonnaise should

curdle, pour it into a jug, add one more egg to the liquidizer and at slowest speed pour in the curdled mayonnaise in a thin trickle. This will regain a smooth, thick mayonnaise.

Mustard Cream Sauce

Mix seasoning, made mustard and lemon juice into whipped cream to make a speedy mustard sauce to serve with steak, beef, herrings or Vienna sausages.

Serves 4 to 6

INGREDIENTS

2 oz. double cream or tinned cream
shake of pepper
¼ teaspoon salt

1 teaspoon made English mustard
1 teaspoon lemon juice or more to taste

METHOD

1 Whisk cream lightly.
2 Add seasonings, mustard and lemon juice and stir to blend.

Oniony Gravy

For delicious flavour, boil wafer-thin slices of onion in the gravy to serve with a joint of meat.

INGREDIENTS

2 medium onions
drippings from the pan in
   which the joint roasted

water or vegetable water —
   approximately ¾ pint
½ stock cube
1 teaspoon sugar

METHOD

1 Peel the onions and slice them wafer-thin.
2 Dish up the joint and put in the warm while you continue with the next steps to make the gravy.
3 Pour off the surplus fat into your dripping jar or basin.
4 Add vegetable water or, failing that, tap water to the sediment left in the pan. Add the piece of stock cube for extra flavour.
5 Add the onions and bring to the boil, stirring thoroughly.
6 Add the sugar and boil rapidly, stirring, for about 3 or 4 minutes, until the onion slices are tender.
7 Serve hot in a sauceboat and pour over the sliced meat.

Pineapple and Walnut Stuffing

This is an unusual stuffing for a special roast chicken. It is finely chopped, or crushed, canned pineapple and chopped walnuts, mixed with buttery fresh breadcrumbs, moistened with a little pineapple juice.

Sufficient for a 3½–4-lb. chicken

INGREDIENTS

1½ oz. butter
1 teacup fresh white
   breadcrumbs
3 slices canned pineapple, or

3 heaped tablespoons
   crushed pineapple
2 oz. walnuts
little pineapple juice from can

METHOD

1 Melt the butter.
2 Stir in the breadcrumbs.
3 Chop the pineapple finely if necessary.
4 Chop the walnuts.
5 Stir the pineapple and walnuts into the buttery
   breadcrumbs, adding a little pineapple juice if
   necessary to moisten it.
6 Use to pack loosely into the neck or body cavity of
   the bird, or both.

Sausage-Meat and Chestnut Stuffing

For roast turkey, some people like sausage-meat stuffing,
others chestnut. This combines the two, with apples and
onions for extra flavour. This quantity is sufficient for the
neck and body cavity of a 10-lb. ready-to-cook turkey.

INGREDIENTS

1 lb. sausage-meat
½ 15-oz. can unsweetened
  chestnut purée
1 large onion, peeled and
  chopped
2 medium cooking apples,
  peeled and chopped

4 oz. fresh breadcrumbs
1 large egg + 1 yolk (or 2
  small eggs), beaten
salt and pepper
turkey liver (optional), cut up

METHOD

Mix all ingredients together and use to stuff the body cavity or neck of the turkey, or some in each. Do not stuff too tightly: the heat must penetrate to cook the stuffing thoroughly.

Yorkshire Pudding with Herbs

Contrary to what most recipes say, it is not necessary to beat the batter till it is foaming with air, or to leave it for half an hour to rest before cooking. It will rise perfectly well if the beaten egg and milk are merely stirred into the flour. The heat of the oven is sufficient to convert the liquid in the recipe to steam, so that the Yorkshire pudding rises. Mixed dried herbs add flavour which goes well with roast beef.

Serves 6 or makes 8 popovers

Oven temperature: 400°F, gas mark 6

Cooking time: 30–40 minutes

INGREDIENTS

4 oz. plain flour	8 fluid oz. milk
½ teaspoon salt	1 teaspoon herbs
1 to 2 eggs (2 eggs gives a richer batter)	cooking fat or beef drippings (approximately 2 oz.)

METHOD

1   Sift the flour and salt into a bowl.
2   Beat the eggs, add the milk and herbs and combine thoroughly.
3   Make a well in the centre of the dry ingredients, pour in sufficient of the liquid to mix to a smooth, medium-thick paste.
4   Add the remaining liquid and stir with a wooden spoon until well blended.
5   Melt the cooking fat or drippings in a Yorkshire pudding tin (a deep roasting tin) and when hot pour in the batter. Bake at 400°F, gas mark 6, for 30 to 40 minutes until well risen and brown. At this stage the oven heat can be turned off and the Yorkshire pudding dried off in the oven for 5 to 10 minutes.

Note: If preferred, the mixture can be baked in ramekins to make individual popovers. The popovers, like the Yorkshire pudding, are served with roast beef.

Chapter 10
Desserts

Apple Jeannette

As a change from baked apple, serve peeled, cored, thinly sliced apples layered in a casserole with demerara sugar and butter.

Serves 4

Oven temperature: 350°F, gas mark 4

Cooking time: approximately 40 minutes

INGREDIENTS

2 lb. Bramley cooking apples   1½ oz. butter
1½ oz. demerara sugar   top milk or cream

METHOD

1   Core, peel, slice and quarter the apple with a sharp knife.
2   Grease an ovenproof dish and put in a layer of apples, a sprinkling of sugar and shavings of butter.

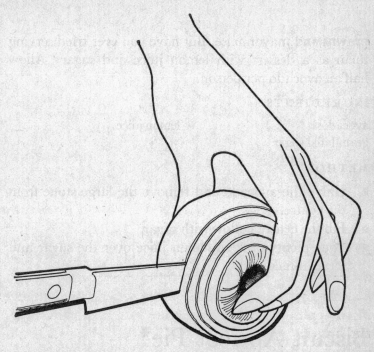

3 Repeat the layers until all the ingredients have been used up.

4 Bake, with the lid on (or covered with foil), at 350°F, gas mark 4, for approximately 40 minutes, until the apples are soft and syrupy.

5 Serve hot with top milk or cream.

Avocado Dessert

Avocados are usually served as an appetizer, with a vinaigrette dressing. They are also delicious stuffed with prawns and mayonnaise. But have you ever tried serving them as a dessert with lemon juice and sugar? Allow half an avocado per person.

INGREDIENTS

avocados   lemon juice
granulated sugar

METHOD

1   Halve the avocado and remove the large stone from the centre.
2   Fill the centre hollow with sugar.
3   Pour plenty of fresh lemon juice over the sugar and serve immediately.

Biscuit Apricot Pie*

Make an apricot pie from quick-cooking ingredients: a biscuit crust instead of pastry and a can of apricot pie filling sharpened and thickened with lemon juice, egg and soured cream or yogurt. It takes only minutes to make and only half an hour to cook. But give it time to cool and chill because it needs to be eaten cold.

Serves 8

✻ This *would* freeze, but I would not recommend it, as the pie filling is already a convenience factor. There is no real point in freezing something that is already preserved in an alternative way.

Oven temperature: 350°F, gas mark 4

Cooking time: 30 minutes

This pie cannot be turned out but needs to be served from the base of the tin. Therefore use an 8½-inch spring-form tin (see illustration on page 192). Alternatively, with care, a loose-bottomed cake tin can be used.

INGREDIENTS

½ lb. digestive biscuits
4 oz. unsalted butter
about 2 tablespoons blanched,
    flaked almonds*
1 can apricot pie filling

1 tablespoon lemon juice
1 egg, beaten
1 carton soured cream or
    yogurt

*Blanched almonds can be bought in packets, ready flaked. If you cannot get them, use nibbed almonds or chop some blanched almonds finely.

METHOD

1   In a medium pan, gently melt the butter. (The other half of the packet of unsalted butter could be used for making Apple Curd, page 215).

2   Meanwhile put the biscuits, a few at a time, in a large paper bag and crush them to crumbs by rolling briskly with a rolling pin.

3   Off the heat, shake all the biscuit crumbs into the melted butter and stir together thoroughly.

4   Press two-thirds of the mixture evenly into the base and slightly up the sides of the tin.

5   Stir the flaked almonds into the rest of the biscuit crust mixture and reserve for the topping.

6 Empty the can of apricot pie filling into a bowl and roughly chop up the apricots if they seem too large. Stir in the lemon juice, beaten egg and soured cream or yogurt.
7 Spoon this mixture into the biscuit-lined tin.
8 Sprinkle thickly with the rest of the biscuit crumbs and almonds, covering all the mixture.
9 Bake on the centre shelf of oven, 350°F, gas mark 4, for 30 minutes.
10 Cool.
11 Remove base from rest of tin and serve the pie from this base. If possible, put in the refrigerator cabinet to become quite cold.

Brandied Peaches

For those who cannot rise to the heights of flambé desserts, this comes a very good second: peaches gently grilled with brown sugar and a little brandy, then transferred to an individual deep dish, more brandy poured over, and the whole topped with whipped cream. Very simple and foolproof.

Serves 4 or more

INGREDIENTS

½ peach, fresh or canned,   brandy
  per person   double cream, whipped
soft brown sugar

METHOD

1 Halve each peach, stone and peel.
2 Fill the centre hollow with soft brown sugar, using only a little sugar for canned peaches.
3 Spoon over a little brandy.
4 Grill gently, without turning, till warmed through (about 10 minutes).
5 Transfer to individual dishes, pour more brandy over (be generous) and top with whipped double cream. Serve warm.

Bread Doughnuts

There is no doughnut mixture to make – merely de-crust a white loaf and cut it into 1½-inch cubes. Dip these swiftly in orange juice and then into beaten egg and deep-fat fry. Drain, then sprinkle with sieved icing sugar mixed with cinnamon. Serve piping hot with warmed jam.

Serves 4

INGREDIENTS

½ large uncut white loaf, de-crusted
approximately ½ pint orange juice
2 eggs, beaten

2 oz. icing sugar, sieved
¼ teaspoon ground cinnamon
oil for deep-fat frying
jam

METHOD

1   Cut the bread into 1½-inch cubes.
2   Quickly dip into orange juice and then into beaten egg.
3   Fry in deep fat till golden brown.
4   Drain on absorbent paper.
5   Sprinkle with icing sugar mixed with the cinnamon.
6   Serve immediately with warmed jam.

Brown Betty

A cold dessert of layers of stewed apple and fried brown (or white) breadcrumbs. Top it with whipped cream and grated chocolate just before serving.

Serves 6

INGREDIENTS

2 lb. cooking apples
caster or granulated sugar
2 oz. butter

3 oz. crumbs of brown or
   white bread
¼ pint double cream, whipped
1 tablespoon grated chocolate

METHOD

1   Peel, core and quarter apples and cook to apple-sauce consistency in just enough water to cook to a mash without burning.
2   Sweeten to taste – it should be slightly tart rather than over-sweet. Cool.
3   Melt the butter in a large pan and fry the crumbs

with a tablespoon of caster sugar till golden and crisp, stirring constantly. Cool.

4 Arrange apple sauce and crumbs in layers, finishing with a layer of apple sauce. Refrigerate if possible.

5 Before serving, decorate with whipped cream and sprinkle with grated chocolate.

Chocolate Pudding with Chocolate Sauce

Orange rind in the pudding and orange juice in the chocolate sauce give a pleasant tangy flavour to this steamed chocolate pudding. It is served with sliced fresh orange.

Serves 6

Steaming time: 1½ hours

You will need a 1½-pint pudding basin and greaseproof paper or foil

INGREDIENTS

4 oz. margarine

4 oz. soft brown sugar

1 oz. cocoa powder

2–3 tablespoons hot water

2 eggs, beaten

6 oz. self-raising flour

grated rind of 1 orange

1 tablespoon milk if necessary

Sauce

4 oz. soft brown sugar

2 oz. cocoa powder

¼ pint water

juice of 1 orange

1 oz. butter

Decoration

1 orange, peeled and sliced

METHOD

1 Beat margarine and sugar together until light and creamy.

2 Blend cocoa powder with hot water and beat into mixture.

3 Gradually add eggs, beating well between each addition.

4 Fold in flour and orange rind.

5 Stir in sufficient milk to give a dropping consistency.

6 Turn mixture into a greased 1½-pint pudding basin and cover with greased greaseproof paper or foil.

7 Steam for 1½ hours.

8 For the sauce, place all ingredients in a saucepan. Heat slowly and stir until sugar has dissolved. Then boil rapidly for 2 to 3 minutes until sauce coats the back of a wooden spoon.

9 Turn pudding out onto serving dish and decorate with halved slices of orange round the edge of the dish. Spoon a little chocolate sauce onto the top of the pudding and serve remaining sauce separately. Serve hot. If only part of the pudding is used, the rest can be put back in the basin, covered and re-steamed for half an hour next day.

Dessert Apple and Cream

Serves 3 or more

INGREDIENTS

1 Cox's apple per person   caster or demerara sugar
single cream or top milk

METHOD

1 Wash the apples. (There is no need to peel unless you wish.) With a sharp knife, cut very thin small slices of the apple onto the serving plate. If you have a slicer and shredder attachment to an electric mixer, quarter and core the apples first, then use the drum which gives wafer-thin slices as for potato crisps.

2 Pour over some single cream or top milk.

3 Sprinkle with sugar to taste.

4 Eat immediately, before the raw apple has time to discolour.

Four-Fruit Pie*

This is a delicious pie to make in late summer or early autumn. It is a mixture of Victoria plums, fresh peaches, cooking pears and cooking apples, sweetened, covered

* The mixture of fruit may be frozen and made into this pie at any time of the year – using frozen pastry too, if you like.

with shortcrust, baked until the fruits are juicy and the pastry rich and golden, and served with fresh cream or ice cream.

Serves 6

Oven temperature: 425°F, gas mark 7

Cooking time: approximately 35 minutes

You will need a deep pie dish

INGREDIENTS

Pastry
Shortcrust pastry (page 182 or 184)

Filling
½ lb. Victoria plums
2 fresh peaches

2 cooking pears
2 small cooking apples
1–2 tablespoons brown sugar
1 tablespoon water
milk and caster sugar to glaze pastry

METHOD

1   Make the shortcrust pastry. According to the size of the pie dish you may need pastry made with 4–6 oz. flour and the fat in proportion. Or make the full quantity of pastry and use the left-overs for tartlets or turnovers.

2   Wash all the fruit. Cut the plums in half and remove stones. Peel, core or stone and slice the peaches, pears and apples. Put all the fruit in the deep pie dish with the sugar and water.

3   Make a rim of pastry round the edge of the dish and then cover the dish with the rolled-out pastry. Brush with milk and sprinkle with caster sugar.

4 Bake at 425°F, gas mark 7, till the fruit is tender and juicy and the pastry is golden (approximately 35 minutes). Serve with fresh cream or ice cream.

Great-Grandmother's Christmas Pudding

This makes three medium-sized puddings. Allow them at least a month to mature. Even if you only need one, make the full quantity – they keep well for a year or two. You will need 3 medium-sized pudding basins

INGREDIENTS

9 oz. plain flour
1 lb. shredded suet
1 lb. white breadcrumbs
1 lb. demerara or soft brown sugar
1 lb. seedless raisins
1 lb. currants
½ lb. sultanas
1–2 oz. ground almonds
2 oz. candied peel

½ nutmeg, grated (or ½ teaspoon grated nutmeg)
1 small teaspoon mixed spice
1 small teaspoon salt
juice and grated rind of 1 small lemon
¼ pint milk
¼ pint brandy
4 eggs, separated

METHOD

1 Wash the raisins, currants and sultanas, pat off excess moisture with kitchen paper and put the fruit to dry in deep roasting tins in a very cool oven, stirring occasionally.

2   Mix together all the ingredients except the whites of
     eggs and leave to stand, covered, for some hours or
     all night.

3   Just before boiling, whisk whites of eggs stiff and mix
     in thoroughly, but as lightly as possible.

4   Fill well-greased basins, allowing a little space at the
     top for puddings to rise. Cover with a circle of
     greased greaseproof paper greased-side down and
     then two thicknesses of kitchen foil.

5   Stand the basin on a trivet, with boiling water coming
     halfway up the sides of the basin. If using aluminium
     pans, put a tablespoon of vinegar in the water to pre-
     vent the pan staining. Cover the pan with a lid and
     boil gently, topping the water up with more boiling
     water from time to time. The puddings need about
     8–9 hours' boiling (alternatively, use a pressure
     cooker, following the manufacturer's instructions).

6   After cooking, re-cover as before with fresh greased
     greaseproof paper and foil and keep till Christmas
     Day. They should have at least a month to mature,
     longer if possible.

7   On Christmas Day, re-boil for at least 2 hours.

Lemon Meringue Pie

There are many favourite recipes for lemon meringue
pie, but this is a particularly smooth and lemony version.

INGREDIENTS
Pastry
see pages 182–5 for recipe

Lemon filling
8 oz. caster sugar
grated rind and juice from 2
   lemons
1 oz. butter
2 egg yolks
$\frac{1}{2}$ pint hot water
4 level tablespoons cornflour

Meringue topping
2 egg whites
2 oz. granulated sugar
2 oz. caster sugar
glacé cherries
angelica
a little extra caster sugar

METHOD

1   Make pastry case following the method on page 183.

2   To make the lemon filling: Place the sugar, grated lemon rind and juice, butter and egg yolks into a saucepan. Stir thoroughly together. Pour in the water and bring to the boil, stirring.

3   In a separate basin, blend the cornflour with a little cold water to a smooth cream.

4   Stir some of the boiling lemon mixture into the cornflour, return it all to the pan and simmer gently for 2 to 3 minutes.

5   Pour into the cooled pastry case and leave to cool slightly.

6   To make the meringue topping: Whisk the egg whites stiffly, add the granulated sugar all at once and whisk again. Gradually fold in the caster sugar.

7   Pile the meringue mixture onto the lemon filling, spreading it roughly over the whole filling to the edges, sealing the filling completely.

8 Decorate with cut glacé cherries and angelica and sprinkle with a little caster sugar.

9 Heat very slowly under a cool grill until the meringue peaks go pale golden, turning the pie to colour all the meringue. *Or*, bake in a pre-heated slow oven 300°F, gas mark 2, for 10 minutes or longer until the meringue turns golden.

10 Serve cold.

Melon in Ginger Ale

Ever since – at a smart restaurant at the age of 18 – I choked on a pinch of dry ginger and the wine waiter had to rush to my rescue with a carafe of water, I have never served powdered ginger with melon. Instead I serve cut-up melon in ginger ale – either as a first course or as a dessert.

INGREDIENTS

honeydew melon
ginger ale

METHOD

1 Cut the melon in half and discard the seeds. If you have a melon ball cutter, scoop out rounds of melon into the individual serving bowls. Alternatively, cut the melon in slices, then cut the flesh into small cubes, discarding the skin.

2 Just before serving, pour fizzy ginger ale over the

melon. This gives the flavour of ginger and a pleasant juice as well.

Mincemeat Charlotte*

This makes a change from the usual apple or fruit charlotte. In this recipe the grated apple is mixed with plenty of mincemeat. The charlotte mixture of breadcrumbs, suet and sugar is flavoured with cinnamon. This charlotte can be used as a lighter alternative to Christmas Pudding.

Serves 4 to 6

Oven temperature: 375°F, gas mark 5

Cooking time: 30 minutes

INGREDIENTS

4 oz. fresh white breadcrumbs	½ lb. mincemeat
2 oz. shredded suet	grated rind and juice of 1
2 oz. demerara sugar	lemon
½ teaspoon cinnamon	cream, top milk or custard
1 lb. cooking apples	(optional)

METHOD

1   Stir together the breadcrumbs, suet, sugar and cinnamon.
2   Into another bowl, grate the peeled, cored apples and combine with the mincemeat.

✳ Freeze after stage 9 and complete cooking later as recommended, allowing 10 minutes' extra cooking time.

3   Add the lemon rind and juice to the apples and mincemeat.

4   Well butter an ovenproof dish, preferably a soufflé dish.

5   Put one-third of the breadcrumb mixture in a layer over the bottom of the dish.

6   Add half the mincemeat mixture.

7   Put in a layer of the next one-third of the breadcrumb mixture.

8   Add the rest of the mincemeat mixture.

9   For the final layer add the last of the breadcrumb mixture.

10 Bake at 375°F, gas mark 5, for 30 minutes.

11 Serve with cream, top milk or custard if desired.

Orange Cornflake Pie

Make an orange chiffon mixture with orange and lemon juice whipped with gelatine, egg white and cream. This can be turned into an uncooked refrigerated pie, using a crisp cornflake pie crust. Alternatively it can be served without the pie crust in individual glasses.

Serves 8

INGREDIENTS

Cornflake pie crust
3½ oz. cornflakes
2½ oz. margarine

2 level teaspoons caster sugar
1 level tablespoon golden syrup

Filling

$\frac{1}{4}$ oz. gelatine ($\frac{1}{2}$ level
  tablespoon)
2 tablespoons cold water
$\frac{1}{4}$ pint orange juice
pinch of salt

$2\frac{1}{2}$ oz. caster sugar
1 tablespoon lemon juice
1 white of egg
$\frac{1}{8}$ pint double cream, whipped

METHOD

1 Put the cornflakes in a large paper or plastic bag and roll them with a rolling pin to crush them medium-fine.

2 Cream the margarine, sugar and syrup together. Add the crushed cornflakes, working in well.

3 Line an 8-inch pie plate with this mixture, pressing down smoothly with a metal spoon and knife.

4 Chill in the food storage compartment of the refrigerator for at least an hour.

5 Soak the gelatine in the water.

6 Bring the orange juice, salt and $1\frac{1}{2}$ oz. of the sugar to the boil.

7 Add the soaked gelatine and stir till dissolved.

8 Add the lemon juice. Cool until the mixture begins to thicken.

9 Whip the white of egg till stiff. Add the remaining 1 oz. sugar and beat again. Fold into the thickening orange jelly.

10 Whip the cream and fold in.

11 Pour into the prepared crust and chill till set firm.

Note: Alternatively, the orange chiffon mixture can be served without the pie crust in individual glasses. If you double the amount of ingredients for the filling you will make about 8 individual chiffons. The 2 egg yolks can be used to enrich scrambled eggs.

Orange Pudding

To make a refreshingly light suet pudding, add grated orange rind to the suet mixture and layer it in the bowl with thin slices of fresh orange. Steam for about 3 hours and serve with a marmalade sauce.

Serves 6

You will need a 2½–3-pint pudding basin

INGREDIENTS

Pudding

4 oz. plain flour
1½ teaspoons baking powder
½ level teaspoon salt
4 oz. fresh white breadcrumbs
3 oz. shredded suet
3 oz. caster sugar
3 oranges

1 egg, beaten
8 tablespoons milk

Sauce

2 level teaspoons cornflour
¼ pint water
4 level tablespoons marmalade
2 teaspoons lemon juice

METHOD

1 Sift flour, baking powder and salt into a bowl and stir in breadcrumbs, suet and caster sugar.
2 Grate rind from 2 of the oranges.

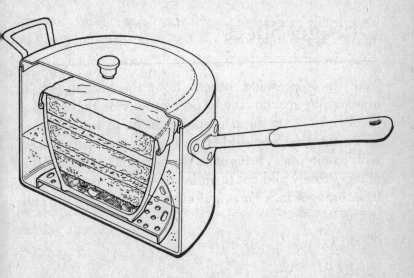

3   Add rind to flour mixture with beaten egg and milk
    and mix to a soft batter.
4   Grease a 2½–3-pint pudding basin.
5   Peel all 3 oranges and cut into ¼-inch thick slices.
    Arrange a few orange slices in bottom of basin.
6   Cover with a layer of the pudding mixture and another
    layer of orange. Repeat layers once more, ending
    with a layer of pudding mixture.
7   Cover with greased foil or greaseproof paper and
    steam for 2¾ to 3 hours.
8   Turn out and serve with sauce. To make sauce, blend
    together cornflour and water in a pan and stir in
    marmalade and lemon juice. Bring to the boil,
    stirring, and simmer for 5 minutes.

Orange Slices

Many people would benefit from the vitamin C in oranges but are too lazy to peel and divide the fruit for themselves. They need encouragement to eat oranges. Grate the rind and add it to a sugar syrup, flavoured with lemon juice. Bring it to the boil. Peel and slice the oranges thinly and cut them up. Pour the syrup over the fresh oranges in a bowl and eat immediately while still warm.

Serves 4

INGREDIENTS

4 small or 2 large oranges   juice of 1 lemon
½ cup granulated sugar

METHOD

1   Wash and dry the oranges. Grate the outer orange rind (or zest) from 1 large or 2 small oranges.
2   Put ½ cup granulated sugar in a small pan.
3   Pour the lemon juice into the emptied cup, fill with water and empty juice and water into the pan.
4   Add the grated orange rind and bring to the boil.
5   Remove all pith and peel from the oranges and cut the fruit across into thin (¼-inch) slices. Cut each slice into bite-sized pieces and put into individual serving bowls.
6   Pour the boiling hot syrup over the oranges and eat immediately.

Ice-Cream Pancakes

Hot, thin pancakes are wrapped round fingers of vanilla ice cream, then sprinkled thickly with grated chocolate and eaten straight away before the ice cream has time to melt. These have to be made one by one for each guest, so we make them and eat them queuing up in the kitchen.

Makes 8 pancakes

INGREDIENTS

4 oz. plain flour	½ pint milk
½ level teaspoon salt	block vanilla ice cream
1 egg	plain chocolate, grated

METHOD

1 Sift flour and salt into a basin, make a well in the centre and crack in the unbeaten egg.
2 Add 1 tablespoon milk and begin to mix smoothly. Add enough milk for a thick batter. Beat with a wooden spoon until the mixture is full of air bubbles and the spoon makes a plopping sound.
3 Stir in the remaining milk, taking care not to expel the air.

With a liquidizer this can be made in 30 seconds. Merely place all batter ingredients except the flour in the goblet. Switch to maximum speed. Remove lid and spoon in the flour. Replace lid and blend for 30 seconds.

4 Heat a knob of lard or a little oil in the bottom of the pancake pan. Pour off, leaving the pan well greased.

5   Pour enough batter into the pan to cover it very
    thinly. Tilt quickly to spread.
6   Cook until the underside browns, loosening all round
    from the pan with a palette knife.
7   Toss or turn and fry the other side.
8   Turn out onto a plate. Cut a finger of ice cream, put
    it on top of the pancake and rapidly roll the pancake
    round it. Sprinkle thickly with grated chocolate and
    eat.

Peach Melba, Simple Method

A simple Melba sauce can be made by heating together
equal quantities of redcurrant jelly (the preserve, not
packet jelly) and water. When the jelly has melted, pour
it over sliced fresh peaches and serve with cream or ice
cream.

Serves any number

INGREDIENTS

1 fresh peach per person   1 tablespoon water per
1 tablespoon redcurrant   person
  jelly per person   cream or vanilla ice cream

METHOD

1   Halve the peaches to remove the stones, if using free-
    stone peaches such as the popular Hale variety. If
    using clingstone peaches the stone cannot be removed
    at this stage.

2   Peel the peaches. If they are difficult to peel, immerse
    them for a couple of minutes in boiling water, then
    cover with cold water and you will find the skin will
    peel off easily.

3   Cut the peaches into slices – with clingstone peaches,
    slice the flesh away from the stone.

4   Heat the jelly and water gently in a small saucepan.
    When the jelly has melted, pour over the peaches.

5   Allow to cool and serve with whipped cream or
    vanilla ice cream.

Pear Belle Hélène with Walnuts

Serve pears and ice cream with hot chocolate sauce,
giving crunch and flavour by adding chopped walnuts
to the sauce.

Serves 4

INGREDIENTS

4 pear halves (fresh or canned)   small knob margarine or
4 oz. plain chocolate   butter
4 tablespoons milk   1 oz. walnuts
                                   block vanilla ice cream

METHOD

1   Peel, halve and core 2 large juicy pears. Or use canned
    pears.

2   Break the chocolate into a heatproof basin or the top of a double boiler.
3   Stand it over a pan of gently simmering water.
4   Add the milk and margarine or butter and stir until the chocolate is just melted.
5   Chop the walnuts and add them to the chocolate sauce.
6   Arrange the pears and ice cream on serving plates, pour over them the hot chocolate walnut sauce and serve at once.

Pear Cassata

Peel, halve and core juicy dessert pears. Into the centre hollow, spoon vanilla ice cream mixed with cut-up glacé cherries, dried walnuts, candied peel and seedless raisins.

Serves 4

INGREDIENTS

2 large or 4 small juicy $\frac{1}{2}$–1 oz. candied peel
   dessert pears   1 oz. seedless raisins
8–10 glacé cherries   block vanilla ice cream
$\frac{1}{2}$–1 oz. walnuts

METHOD

1   Halve the pears, peel and, with a sharp teaspoon, scoop out the centre core.
2   Cut up the cherries and walnuts and mix with the peel and raisins.

3 Just before serving take a portion of ice cream for each
   pear and chop it roughly with the fruit.
4 Fill the hollows of the pear and serve immediately.

Plum or Apple Butter Crisp

As a speedy alternative to making pastry, place stoned,
halved fresh plums – cut side up – on slices of bread
thickly buttered. Strew the plums with soft dark brown
sugar and bake in a moderate oven for about 15 to 20
minutes until the plums are soft and juicy and the bread
is golden and crisp.

Or, with peeled dessert apples, cut across in slices about
$\frac{1}{4}$–$\frac{1}{2}$-inch thick, cut out the core and use the apple rings
in place of plums.

Serves 3

Oven temperature: 325°F, gas mark 3

Cooking time: 15–20 minutes

INGREDIENTS

6 large plums, preferably
   Switzens or Victorias, or
   2–3 dessert apples

3 medium-thick slices white
   bread
butter
soft dark brown sugar

METHOD

1 Wash the plums, cut in half and remove stones. Or

peel dessert apples, cut across in slices and cut out cores.
2   Butter the bread thickly and remove crusts.
3   Place the plums, cut side up – or the apple slices – on the buttered bread and strew the fruit thickly with the sugar.
4   Bake at 325°F, gas mark 3, until the fruit is soft and the bread crisp and golden.

Plum Compôte

The flavour of orange juice blends well with Victoria plums to make this juicy compôte. Allow one orange to each 1 lb. plums.

Serves 4–6

Oven temperature: 300°F, gas mark 2

Cooking time: approximately 30 minutes

INGREDIENTS

2 lb. Victoria plums   approximately 2 oz. soft
2 oranges   brown sugar

METHOD

1   Halve and stone the plums.
2   Place cut side down into a casserole.
3   Strew each layer with soft brown sugar.
4   Squeeze the oranges and pour the juice over the plums.

5   Cover and cook in a slow oven, 300°F, gas mark 2, till
    tender.

Plum Flan

Line an oblong flan tin with a rich shortcrust pastry.
Lay halved Switzen plums, cut side down, in close rows
to cover the pastry. Sprinkle with a crumble of 3 oz. each
of flour, ground almonds, demerara sugar, 2 oz. butter or
margarine and the essence (lightly rubbed together) – or
you can use extra flour instead of the ground almonds.

Serves 8–10

Oven temperature: 400°F, gas mark 6

Cooking time: approximately 30 minutes

INGREDIENTS

Shortcrust pastry using 6 oz.   3 oz. demerara sugar
  flour (see page 182 or 184)   2 oz. butter or margarine
1–1½ lb. Switzen plums   2–3 drops almond essence
3 oz. flour ⎤   cream or yogurt
3 oz. ground ⎬ or 6 oz. flour
  almonds   ⎦

METHOD

1   Roll the pastry to line an oblong flan tin.
2   Cover all over with halved stoned plums, placed in
    rows cut side down.
3   Rub the crumble ingredients together lightly until

they resemble fine breadcrumbs. Sprinkle the crumble over the plums.

4   Bake at 400°F, gas mark 6, until golden brown, approximately 30 minutes. Serve hot or cold with cream or yogurt.

Rhubarb with Blackcurrant Drink

The flavour of blackcurrant drink or juice goes well with rhubarb. Make sure to use one that is rich in vitamin C. The recipe needs no sugar because the blackcurrant syrup is sweet enough to counteract the sourness of the rhubarb.

Serves 3 or 4

INGREDIENTS

1 lb. rhubarb   4 tablespoons blackcurrant
                                                        drink

METHOD

1   Discard the rhubarb leaves and wash and cut the rhubarb into small pieces, about an inch long.
2   Pour on some boiling water and leave for 10 minutes before draining off the water.
3   Put the drained rhubarb into a saucepan and pour on the blackcurrant drink. Put on the lid.
4   Cook gently till softened (approximately 10 minutes).

Rhubarb with Banana

You may prefer the mild flavour of banana to the strong flavour of blackcurrant with rhubarb. Treat the rhubarb in the same way as in the preceding recipe, but leave about a dessertspoon of water behind when draining. Simmer until softened (approximately 10 minutes). Add raw sliced banana and sugar to taste. Serve warm or cold.

Rhubarb Tart*

To prevent soft, soggy pastry when making rhubarb tart, sprinkle the pastry with ground almonds or biscuit crumbs, before putting on the pieces of rhubarb. Fill in the gaps with more ground almonds or crumbs and sprinkle liberally with sugar before baking.

Serves 5 or 6

Oven temperature: 400°F, gas mark 6

Cooking time: approximately 30 minutes

INGREDIENTS

- shortcrust pastry made with 6 oz. flour
- 2 oz. ground almonds or biscuit crumbs
- 1 lb. rhubarb, cut in small pieces
- 2 oz. granulated sugar
- cream (optional)

* Freeze after stage 4, omitting the sugar. Complete cooking later by thawing, then adding sugar, and bake as indicated.

METHOD

1   Make your favourite shortcrust recipe (see below and page 184 for two examples) or buy ready-prepared shortcrust pastry. Roll it out thinly and use to line a Swiss roll tin or baking sheet.

2   Sprinkle with some of the ground almonds, or roll biscuits with a rolling pin to make crumbs.

3   Place raw fruit pieces in neat rows.

4   Fill in the gaps with more ground almonds or crumbs. Sprinkle liberally with sugar.

5   Bake at 400°F, gas mark 6, for approximately 30 minutes.

6   Serve hot, with cream if liked.

Shortcrust Pastry (1)

This is a melt-in-the-mouth pastry because it uses more fat or shortening than the normal shortcrust. It has to be handled gently because of the high proportion of fat, and is easier to roll if it is left in the cool (e.g. a refrigerator cabinet) for an hour or so. Or it can be made a day or two before you want it, as long as you give it time to thaw out before it is rolled.

Oven temperature for a pastry case: 375°F, gas mark 5

Cooking time for a pastry case: 30–40 minutes

If you are using this pastry to make a one-crust tart you will need a 7–8-inch pie plate or sandwich tin, or an 8-

inch flan ring; also greaseproof paper and dried beans or peas for weighing the pastry down while it is cooking.

INGREDIENTS

8 oz. plain flour
½ teaspoon salt
3 oz. margarine (not soft variety)

3 oz. cooking fat
2 tablespoons water

METHOD

1 Sieve the flour and salt into a bowl and gently rub in the cut-up margarine and cooking fat until the mixture looks like breadcrumbs.

2 Mix in the water to form a firm dough and knead very lightly for a few seconds to make a round ball without cracks in it.

3 At this stage if you flour the rolling pin well you can roll the pastry out straight away, but it is easier to wrap it in floured foil and let it rest in the refrigerator cabinet for an hour or more.

4 Remove from refrigerator, give it ¼ hour or so to warm up a little, roll it into a round a little larger than the pie plate, sandwich tin or flan ring.

5 Lift the pastry onto the rolling pin, place over the plate, tin or ring and carefully press down smoothly. Cut off surplus pastry with a sharp knife and use to decorate the edge of the plate if wanted. (I use a small heart-shaped cutter to cut out the decorations.)

6 Prick the pastry. Line the inside of the pastry case with a round of greaseproof paper and arrange baking beans (e.g. butter beans or dried peas) on top to prevent the pastry from rising. Some people merely take

a new, unwrinkled piece of foil and press that on
without using weights.

7 Bake in the pre-heated oven for 15 to 20 minutes.
Carefully lift out the greaseproof paper and beans (or
foil). Return to the oven and bake for a further 15 to
20 minutes or until the pastry is cooked. Leave to
cool.

Note: The recipe given, using 8 oz. flour, is in fact
sufficient for a two-crust tart. If you are making a one-
crust tart you will have some pastry over. I generally use
it for making a few small tartlet cases or a mincemeat
turnover.

Shortcrust Pastry (2)

Shortcrust pastry (1) calls for very light handling of the
ingredients. If you find it difficult to handle pastry
lightly, this second method is a better one for you. Unlike
most pastry recipes, it even calls for thorough kneading.

INGREDIENTS

8 oz. flour   2 tablespoons water
5 oz. margarine

METHOD

1 Use margarine which has been brought to room
temperature for at least an hour. If using soft margarine, do not allow to become too soft.

2   With a fork, cream together one-third of the flour
    with the margarine and water until just mixed ($\frac{1}{2}$
    minute).
3   Stir in the remaining flour to form a firm dough.
4   Knead thoroughly until very smooth. Unlike rubbed-
    in pastry, this kneading will not toughen the pastry
    but will improve it.
5   Use as required (see method 1 for baking blind, or it
    can be used without baking blind to make filled pies
    or tarts).

Stewed Apples*

To cook apples to a fluffy purée, peel and core them and remember to cut them large – in quarters rather than in
small pieces. Do not add any sugar until the end of
cooking – they should be cooked in a little water only.

Conversely, if you want to keep apple segments in shape while
they are cooking, cut the peeled, cored apples small and
cook them in sugar syrup, i.e. sugar dissolved in water.

In this recipe the aim is a fluffy purée. So the apples
are cut large, stewed in just enough water to prevent
burning, flavoured with lemon peel and raisins or sultanas and sweetened to taste when they are hot.

Serves 4

✳ Suitable for freezing.

INGREDIENTS

2 lb. cooking apples
a few tablespoons water
1 lemon

2 oz. sultanas or seedless
   raisins
granulated sugar
cream or top milk

METHOD

1   Quarter the apples, core and peel. Put in a saucepan with a few tablespoons water.

2   Add 4 or 5 strips of the yellow part only of the lemon rind.

3   Wash the sultanas or raisins in hot water to plump them and add to the apples.

4   With the lid tightly on the pan, stew gently until the apples soften and become fluffy. Glance occasionally to make sure there is enough water to cook the apples without burning and to see when they are done. Cooking time will vary with the variety of apple; it is generally about 10 to 15 minutes.

5   Sweeten to taste.

6   Remove the lemon rind before serving the apples, hot or cold, with cream or top of milk.

Two-Fruit Salad

Fresh fruits which blend well together are bananas with peaches, pears, dessert plums, oranges or blackberries. Or choose any other combination of two raw fruits which appeals to you. Pour over a hot sugar syrup, flavoured with orange or lemon peel. Allow to cool before serving.

Serves any number

INGREDIENTS

For 4 people allow, e.g.,
4 fresh peaches, peeled and
   sliced
2 bananas, peeled and sliced

yellow rind of 1 orange or
   lemon, without pith
½ cup granulated sugar
½ cup water

METHOD

1 Prepare the fruit, while making the syrup.
2 Shave off slices of the yellow part only (i.e. zest) of the orange or lemon rind.
3 In a small saucepan, bring the sugar, water and rind to the boil, stirring constantly.
4 Boil for 5 minutes. Discard the rind.
5 Pour the hot syrup over the fruit and put aside to cool or chill.

Chapter 11
Cakes and Biscuits

Brack*

Dried fruit is usually washed and then dried well before use in a cake because wet fruit sinks. But in this traditional fruit loaf, the fruit does not sink even though it is soaked with sugar in tea overnight and a beaten egg and sieved flour are added to the wet mixture. The brack is baked in a loaf tin and when cold is sliced thinly and spread with butter. If wrapped in foil, the uncut brack keeps moist and fresh for a week or more.

Oven temperature: 325°F, gas mark 3

Cooking time: 1–2 hours, depending on the shape of the tin. The best tin to use is a 2-lb. loaf tin, greased

❄ To freeze, wrap in foil when quite cold. To serve, either thaw for 2 to 3 hours at room temperature, or put in oven at 300°F, gas mark 2, for about 30 minutes. The latter gives a better result, but it may then stale more quickly.

INGREDIENTS

½ pint strained tea   1 egg
1 lb. mixed dried fruit   2 (½-pint) cups self-raising
1 (½-pint) cup brown sugar   flour

METHOD

First Day

1 Pour the warm strained tea over the fruit and sugar in
   a mixing bowl. Stir, cover and leave overnight.

Second Day

2 Beat well with the egg and flour. The mixture is a
   soft dropping consistency.

3 Transfer to the prepared tin and bake at 325°F, gas
   mark 3, until it is firm, coming away from the sides
   of the tin, and a skewer pushed into the centre comes
   out clean. This may take from 1 to 2 hours according
   to your oven and the size of the tin.

4 Cool on a wire rack. Slice thinly and serve spread
   with butter.

Butter Biscuits*

These are rich biscuits made by rubbing butter into
flour, cinnamon and sugar, and kneading with the yolk

❋ Will freeze, but should not be stored more than about 6
   weeks because of the high proportion of butter.

of an egg. After pressing thinly into tins they are brushed with egg white and sprinkled with chopped almonds. There is no trouble of rolling out or shaping – the thin layers of biscuit are merely cut into fingers or squares.

Oven temperature: 375°F, gas mark 5

Cooking time: 20–30 minutes

You will need well-greased baking sheets

INGREDIENTS

8 oz. plain flour   1 standard egg, separated
1 level teaspoon cinnamon   1 oz. blanched almonds,
6 oz. caster sugar   finely chopped
6 oz. butter

METHOD

1 Sift the flour and cinnamon into a bowl. Stir in the sugar.
2 Rub in the butter.
3 Stir in the beaten egg yolk and knead lightly.
4 With the thumbs and palms of the hands, press a thin layer into the tins. It may help to spread the surface smoothly with a knife.
5 Brush over with a little lightly beaten white of egg. Sprinkle evenly with the chopped almonds.
6 Bake at 375°F, gas mark 5, until just beginning to colour (about 20 to 30 minutes).
7 Leave for a couple of minutes, then cut into fingers or squares. Remove from the tin when cool.

Stella's Cheesecake

Of all the cheesecakes I have tried, this is the simplest to make. There is not the trouble of pastry-making – this one uses crushed digestive biscuits. The filling is curd cheese, single cream, melted butter, vanilla sugar and beaten eggs.

Serves 10

Oven temperature: 375°F, gas mark 5

Cooking time: 25 minutes

You need an 8½-inch loose-bottomed cake tin or a spring-form tin (see page 192).

INGREDIENTS

butter for greasing tin
4 or 5 digestive biscuits
2 large eggs, beaten
1½ lb. curd cheese (not cream cheese)
4 oz. single cream

1 tablespoon melted butter
6 level tablespoons vanilla sugar, or 6 level tablespoons caster sugar and 3 drops vanilla

METHOD

1 Well butter the bottom of an 8½-inch loose-bottomed cake tin or spring-form tin.
2 Put the digestive biscuits in a large plastic or paper bag and use a rolling pin to crush them to coarse crumbs. Sprinkle two-thirds of the crumbs onto the buttered tin.

3 Mix together the eggs, cheese, cream, butter and vanilla sugar and spoon onto the crumbs.
4 Sprinkle the rest of the crumbs on top.

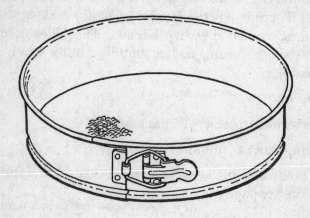

5 Bake at 375°F, gas mark 5, for 25 minutes. It will still seem soft. Allow to cool and eat on the same day, or put in the refrigerator, where it will keep for 2 or 3 days. Do not remove from the tin until cold. Serve on the cake tin base.

Note: Vanilla sugar is expensive to buy. To make it economically at home, take a glass jar with a tightly fitting lid and fill it with caster sugar. Insert a vanilla pod. Very shortly the sugar will take on the flavour of the vanilla. The same vanilla pod can be used over and over again.

Cherry Shortbread

This classic shortbread is made more attractive by the addition of finely chopped glacé cherries. When cool it is cut into pieces and decorated with cut-up glacé cherries.

Serves 8–10

Oven temperature: 325°F, gas mark 3

Cooking time: approximately 40–45 minutes

INGREDIENTS

4 oz. butter
2 oz. caster sugar
5 oz. plain flour
1 oz. fine ground rice

1 oz. finely chopped glacé cherries
glacé cherries (to decorate)

METHOD

1 Put the butter and sugar on a board or in a large bowl, and work with the hand until thoroughly incorporated.
2 Sieve the flour and ground rice together and gradually work, with the cherries, into the butter and sugar until the dough resembles shortcrust pastry.
3 Press with the hand into a round cake approximately 6 inches wide and $\frac{1}{2}$ inch deep. It is easy to lift it on to an ungreased baking sheet either by using a fish slice, or by pressing it first onto greaseproof paper then upending it onto the baking sheet and peeling off the paper.

4   Pinch the edges neatly with finger and thumb. Prick
    the shortbread all over with a fork.
5   Bake in the centre of a very moderate oven, 325°F,
    gas mark 3, until a very pale brown, approximately
    40–45 minutes. Mark into 8 or 10 wedges.
6   Allow to cool a little before cutting into the wedges
    and removing onto a wire tray. Decorate with glacé
    cherries cut in halves or quarters.

Chocolate Cake*

This cake rises with a light texture because the yolks and
whites are separated and the whisked egg whites are
folded gently into the mixture just before baking. The
icing is the simplest of chocolate icings and easy to spread
onto the cake with a knife.

Oven temperature : 350°F, gas mark 4

Cooking time : 50–60 minutes

You will need an 8-inch to 9-inch cake tin

INGREDIENTS

$4\frac{1}{2}$ oz. butter
$7\frac{1}{2}$ oz. caster sugar
1 rounded teaspoon vanilla
    sugar (or 3 drops vanilla)
3 standard eggs, separated

5 oz. plain flour
2 rounded teaspoons baking
    powder
2 rounded tablespoons cocoa
$\frac{1}{8}$ pint or less warm water

* Freeze at stage 6. Ice after thawing.

Chocolate icing

4 oz. plain chocolate
1 oz. butter

METHOD

1 Grease and flour the tin.
2 Cream butter, sugar and vanilla sugar or essence thoroughly together till pale and fluffy.
3 Beat in the egg yolks one at a time.
4 Sift together the flour, baking powder and cocoa and fold lightly in, adding a little water to keep to a fairly stiff dropping consistency.
5 Whisk the egg whites till fairly stiff and gently fold into cake mixture.
6 Turn into the prepared tin and bake at 350°F, gas mark 4, for 50 to 60 minutes till well risen, firm to the touch and just coming away from the sides of the tin.
7 When cool, ice with chocolate icing: melt the chocolate and butter together in a basin over hot water, stir well and spread over the cake.

Chocolate Torte

This moist chocolate cake is made by melting together butter and plain chocolate, adding sugar, egg yolks, vanilla essence and potato flour. The stiffly beaten egg whites are folded in. The cake is spread with raspberry jam and glazed with melted chocolate and butter, flavoured with rum.

Oven temperature: 350°F, gas mark 4

Cooking time: approximately 45 minutes

You will need an 8-inch tin

INGREDIENTS

6 oz. plain chocolate
4 oz. butter
4 oz. caster sugar
4 standard eggs, separated
1 teaspoon vanilla essence
2 oz. potato flour or cornflour
1 teaspoon baking powder
pinch of salt

Glazing

raspberry jam
4 oz. plain chocolate
2 oz. butter
1 tablespoon rum

METHOD

1 Grease the tin, and cover the bottom with a circle of greased greaseproof paper or ungreased bakewell vegetable parchment.
2 Melt the chocolate and butter over hot water.
3 Add the sugar, egg yolks and vanilla essence.
4 Sift and fold in the potato flour and baking powder.
5 Beat the egg whites stiff with a pinch of salt and fold gently into the mixture, which will be a slack batter.
6 Pour into the prepared tin and bake at 350°F, gas mark 4, for approximately 45 minutes, until risen, firm to the touch and just coming away from the sides of the tin.
7 Turn out to cool.
8 Spread the top with raspberry jam.

9 Melt the chocolate and butter over hot water, add
   the rum and pour over the cake, spreading if necessary
   with a knife. Allow to set.

Crispie Biscuits

This is a mixture of warm butter, honey and sugar with
cornflakes. They are baked in an oblong tin and cut into
bars or squares while still warm.

Makes about 12

Oven temperature: 325°F, gas mark 3

Cooking time: approximately 30 minutes

You will need an oblong tin approximately $7 \times 11 \times 1\frac{1}{4}$
inches

INGREDIENTS

3 oz. butter   3 level tablespoons demerara
3 tablespoons clear honey   sugar
                                4 oz. cornflakes

METHOD

1 Heat butter, honey and sugar gently together in a
   small pan until the butter and sugar have melted.
2 Stir this mixture into cornflakes until they are
   thoroughly coated.
3 Butter the tin and turn the cornflake mixture into it.
4 Bake at 325°F, gas mark 3, for about 30 minutes.
5 Cool slightly, loosen the edge with a knife and cut

into bars or squares while still warm. Remove from
the tin with a palette knife.

Currant Biscuits*

Butter and sugar are creamed together and the eggs,
flour and currants or cut-up sultanas are stirred in.
Teaspoons of the mixture are dropped, well apart, onto
a greased baking sheet.

Makes 30 biscuits

Oven temperature: 375°F, gas mark 5

Cooking time: approximately 10–15 minutes

INGREDIENTS

scant 4½ oz. butter
3¾ oz. granulated sugar
2 standard eggs, beaten
4 oz. plain flour, sifted

2 tablespoons currants or
  cut-up sultanas
2 tablespoons brandy
  (optional) or a few drops
  of almond essence

METHOD

1   Cream the butter and sugar till pale and fluffy.
2   Beat in the eggs, flour, currants, and brandy.
3   Put teaspoons of the mixture well apart, on greased
    baking sheets. Bake at 375°F, gas mark 5, till pale
    golden (approximately 10–15 minutes).

❋ Suitable for freezing.

Danish Orange Cake

This is a simple, plain cake made moist by pouring on to the lukewarm cake a fresh orange syrup. The syrup is made by boiling together with a teacup of sugar the juice and grated rind of two oranges and one lemon. The syrup soaks into the cake while it cools, leaving the grated rind to decorate the top.

Oven temperature: 375°F, gas mark 5

Cooking time: approximately 50 minutes

You will need an 8–9-inch cake tin, greased and floured

INGREDIENTS

8 oz. butter	2 large oranges
8 oz. granulated sugar	1 lemon
3 standard eggs	1 teacup granulated sugar
8 oz. self-raising flour	

METHOD

1 Cream the butter and 8 oz. sugar together till pale and fluffy.
2 Beat in the eggs one by one, adding a tablespoon or so of the flour if there are any signs of curdling.
3 Lightly fold in the sifted flour.
4 Turn into the prepared cake tin and bake at 375°F, gas mark 5, for approximately 50 minutes, till risen and golden and coming away from the sides of the tin. Turn onto a cake rack.
5 Grate the rinds of the oranges and lemon. Squeeze

all the juice. Place rind and juice in a small pan, add
the sugar and boil to dissolve.

6   Put the cake on its cake rack over a plate. Pour the
warm fruit syrup over the lukewarm cake, pricking
with a skewer if necessary to help the cake to absorb
all the syrup. The syrup soaks in and the peel
decorates the surface. Any syrup which runs down
onto the plate should be re-poured over the cake.

7   Leave to cool.

Date and Walnut Cake*

As a change from the usual fruit cake make a good-
keeping, cut-and-come-again cake, using dates and
walnuts.

Oven temperature: 350°F, gas mark 4

Cooking time: 1–1¼ hours

You will need a 2-lb. loaf tin or a 7–8-inch round tin
greased and lined with greased greaseproof paper

INGREDIENTS

6 oz. packet dates   2 large eggs, beaten
pinch of bicarbonate of soda   8 oz. self-raising flour, sieved
2 oz. walnuts   apricot jam
5 oz. margarine   few walnut halves for
4 oz. caster sugar   decoration

✳ Freeze before brushing over with jam. Finish as suggested
after thawing.

METHOD

1 Grease and line the tin with greased greaseproof paper. Or use a non-stick tin.
2 Chop the block of dates, then soak them in hot water with a pinch of bicarbonate of soda in the water.
3 Grate some of the 2 oz. walnuts and chop the rest.

4 Cream the margarine and sugar until light and fluffy.
5 Add the beaten eggs a little at a time, with a tablespoon or so of the flour if necessary to prevent curdling.
6 Stir in the rest of the flour.
7 Drain the dates and pat dry with kitchen paper. Add to the cake mixture.

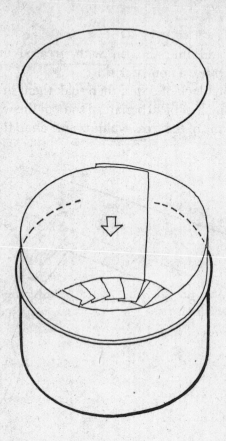

8 Stir in the nuts.
9 Place in the cake tin, smoothing the top, and bake at
   350°F, gas mark 4, for 1–1¼ hours.
10 Turn out on a cooling rack but while still warm
   brush over with apricot jam and decorate with dried
   walnuts. Allow to cool before storing in an airtight
   tin.

Browned Butter Biscuits*

A melt-in-the-mouth biscuit with the subtle flavouring of browned butter and vanilla. They can easily be made with an electric mixer – add the flour at low speed. Brown the butter an hour or more before you make the biscuits to give it time to cool.

Makes 34 biscuits

Oven temperature: 250°F, gas mark $\frac{1}{2}$–1

Cooking time: 30–35 minutes

INGREDIENTS

4 oz. butter
3 oz. (scant) granulated sugar
$\frac{1}{2}$ teaspoon vanilla essence

$\frac{1}{2}$ teaspoon baking powder
$4\frac{1}{2}$ oz. (scant) plain flour
17 blanched almonds

METHOD

1   In a saucepan heat the butter gently until it just begins to brown.
2   Immediately transfer it to the mixing bowl and stand the bowl in cold water until the butter cools and stiffens.
3   Cream the butter and sugar together until fluffy.
4   Add the vanilla essence.
5   Beat in the baking powder and flour.
6   Knead the dough until smooth.
7   With the hands, roll into small balls the size of marbles.

✻ Suitable for freezing.

8 Place on lightly greased baking tins, slightly apart as
   they will spread a little.
9 Press on an almond cut in half.
10 Bake at 250°F, gas mark ½–1, until golden – 30–35
   minutes.

Gingerbread

This is an easy-to-make gingerbread, with several ways
of ringing the changes on the basic recipe so that it is not
always the same.

Oven temperature: 300°F, gas mark 2

Cooking time: 1¼–1½ hours

This quantity of mixture is suitable for any of the following tins: 7-inch or 8-inch square or round cake tins, or
two 7-inch square tins, 1 inch in depth. Prepare by
greasing and bottom-lining.

INGREDIENTS

4 oz. margarine
6 oz. black treacle (6 level
   tablespoons)
2 oz. golden syrup (2 level
   tablespoons)
¼ pint milk
2 standard eggs

8 oz. plain flour
2 oz. sugar
2 level teaspoons mixed spice
3 level teaspoons ground
   ginger
1 level teaspoon bicarbonate
   of soda

Ring the changes with :

1   1 oz. each sultanas, crystallized ginger and shredded almonds *or*
2   4 oz. dried figs, cut in small pieces *or*
3   4 oz. chopped dates *or*
4   4 oz. wholemeal flour in place of 4 oz. plain flour

METHOD

1   In a large saucepan, warm together margarine, treacle and syrup. Add milk and allow to cool.
2   Beat eggs and blend with cooled mixture.
3   Sieve dry ingredients together into a bowl, add the cooled mixture and stir in with a tablespoon. Add fruit if required.
4   Turn into greased and lined tin.
5   Bake on middle shelf at 300°F, gas mark 2, for $1\frac{1}{4}$ to $1\frac{1}{2}$ hours, depending on the size of tin.
6   Serve hot with apple sauce as a pudding, or cold with butter for tea.

Loop Biscuits*

The yolk of a hard-boiled egg is mashed with a raw egg yolk, sugar is added and the mixture is worked to a dough with butter and flour (the quantities are unusual because this is a direct translation of grammes in Norwegian). The

* Suitable for freezing.

dough is rolled into long thin fingers and shaped into loops. These are dipped into egg white beaten with a little water and then into granulated sugar before baking in a moderate oven for about 10 to 15 minutes.

Makes approximately 25–30 biscuits

Oven temperature: 350°F, gas mark 4

Cooking time: approximately 20 minutes

INGREDIENTS

2 standard eggs
1¾ oz. granulated sugar
7 oz. plain flour

4¼–4½ oz. butter (at room temperature)
extra granulated sugar for decoration

METHOD

1 Hard-boil one egg and let it cool. Remove yolk and mash with the yolk of the raw egg. (Eat the hard-boiled egg white – that is cook's 'perks'!)

2 Add the sugar and stir well.

3 Add the sieved flour and the butter (at room temperature, not straight from the fridge) and work together to form a dough.

4 Roll into long thin rolls (the thickness of the little finger of a fairly slim person). Cut into 5½-inch lengths and form into loops.

5 Whisk the remaining raw egg white with one dessert-spoon of water. Brush the loops on one side with egg white and then dip into a plate of granulated sugar, or, if you find this tricky, sprinkle the sugar thickly over the top of the biscuits. This makes an attractive top finish.

6 Bake, slightly apart, at 350°F, gas mark 4, until just turning golden (about 20 minutes).

Puff Pastry Pinwheels

Puff pastry is rolled thin, spread with apricot jam and dried fruit, then rolled up like a Swiss roll. It is scored across the top of the roll to mark into biscuits before baking.

Makes approximately 24 pinwheels

Oven temperature: 400°F, gas mark 6

Cooking time: approximately 20 minutes

INGREDIENTS

1 (7½-oz.) packet puff pastry	currants
apricot jam	milk
sultanas	icing sugar

METHOD

1 Cut the puff pastry into quarters. Roll each quarter thinly to an oblong approximately 7 × 5 inches.

2 Spread thinly with apricot jam. Sprinkle – not too thickly – with sultanas and currants.

3 Roll up lengthwise like a Swiss roll, sealing the edge with water and trimming the ends.

4 Brush with milk. With a knife mark into 6 biscuits approximately 1 inch wide.

5 Bake at 400°F, gas mark 6, for approximately 20 minutes until pale golden.

6 Remove from the oven and dust with icing sugar. Cut through the marks to make 6 pinwheels from each roll.

Refrigerator Biscuits*

These are prepared in advance. The raw mixture is formed into a smooth roll and left to chill in the cabinet of the refrigerator for several hours, overnight or even for a few days. They are then ready for unexpected guests because the roll merely needs to be sliced thinly and baked for 8 to 10 minutes.

Makes approximately 24 biscuits

✻ These may be stored, as suggested, equally well in a freezer. Wrap in foil or freezer wrap. Thaw just sufficiently to cut before baking.

Oven temperature: 400°F, gas mark 6

Cooking time: 8–10 minutes

You will need kitchen foil or a polythene bag

INGREDIENTS

3 oz. butter or margarine
3 oz. caster sugar
1 egg, beaten
6 oz. self-raising flour
¾ teaspoon vanilla essence
   or

grated rind of lemon
   or
1 level teaspoon mixed spice
   or
½ oz. cocoa powder (in place
   of ½ oz. of the flour)

METHOD

1 Cream the butter and sugar till light.
2 Beat in the egg, with the vanilla essence or lemon rind if used.
3 Stir in the sieved flour, with mixed spice or cocoa powder if used.
4 Form into a roll about 2 inches diameter. It is soft at this stage, but do not add any flour to stiffen it, just use a lightly floured board to form it into the roll.
5 Wrap smoothly in kitchen foil or a polythene bag and place in the refrigerator.
6 When needed, cut the number required with a sharp knife into biscuits ¼ inch thick and place well apart on a baking tin. The rest of the dough can be put back in the refrigerator till needed.
7 Bake at 400°F, gas mark 6, for 8 to 10 minutes. Cool.

Rhubarb Queen Cakes*

Queen cakes are usually made with sultanas. For a change replace the sultanas with cut-up fresh raw rhubarb.

Makes 12 to 16

Oven temperature: 375°F, gas mark 5

Cooking time: 15–20 minutes

You need paper cases or patty tins

INGREDIENTS

4 oz. rhubarb	2 standard eggs
4 oz. butter or margarine	4 oz. self-raising flour
4 oz. caster sugar	milk if necessary

METHOD

1 Place 12 to 16 paper cases on baking trays, or grease patty pans.
2 Cut the rhubarb into small cubes, the size of currants or sultanas.
3 Cream the fat and sugar until pale and fluffy.
4 Add the eggs one at a time, beating well and adding a tablespoon or so of flour to avoid curdling.
5 Fold in the rest of the flour. It may be sometimes necessary to add a little milk to make a dropping consistency.
6 Stir in the rhubarb pieces.

❋ Suitable for freezing.

7 Two-thirds fill the paper cases or patty pans with the mixture and bake at 375°F, gas mark 5, till risen and golden (about 15 to 20 minutes).

Electric-Mixer Sponge Cake*

A sponge cake can be made heavy by over-whisking when using an electric mixer but this cake is always light and high rising because the beating is carefully timed. A quick cake to prepare and bake. Use either a stand or hand-held mixer.

Serves 8

Oven temperature: 400°F, gas mark 6

Cooking time: 15 minutes

You will need two 8-inch sandwich tins

INGREDIENTS

4 large eggs
4 oz. caster sugar
4 drops vanilla
4 oz. self-raising flour

jam (or raspberries, strawberries or redcurrants tossed in sugar)
double cream, whipped
icing sugar

METHOD

1 Grease and flour the 2 tins.
2 Separate the whites from the yolks of the eggs.

❋ Freeze before filling. Allow 2 to 3 hours to thaw out at room temperature, then fill as described.

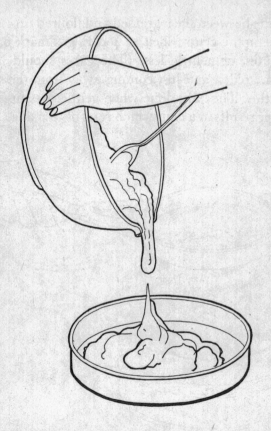

3 With the electric mixer, whisk the egg whites till very frothy but not stiff.

4 Add the yolks and whisk till just beaten in.

5 Add the caster sugar and vanilla. Whisk on highest speed for 5 minutes. The mixture will be foamy and creamy.

6 By hand, gradually and lightly sift in and fold in the flour.

7 Divide between the 2 greased and floured tins.
8 Bake on the centre shelf at 400°F, gas mark 6, for 15 minutes, or a little less. (The cakes should be well risen, golden and just coming away from the sides of the tins. They are done when gentle pressure by the finger results in a dent which returns to shape again.)

9 Turn out onto cake racks. When cold, sandwich together with jam or sugared fruit and whipped double cream.
10 Sift a little icing sugar over the top through a doyley. Lift doyley gently to leave the icing sugar decoration.

Chapter 12
Preserves

Apple Curd*

This is very similar to lemon curd but it has the additional flavour and texture of pulped apple. It is an excellent way to use windfall apples. Spread it on bread and butter or use as a filling for tarts and flans, but remember – because it is so rich with eggs – this apple curd may only keep for about a week or 10 days.

Makes approximately 2 lb.

Allow about 50 minutes for preparation and cooking time; the curd must be stirred until really thickened.

INGREDIENTS

1 lb. cooking apples or windfalls

4 oz. unsalted butter

4 lemons (grated rind and juice)

1 lb. caster sugar

4 eggs (beaten)

❋ If poured into freezable containers, this may be frozen and will then keep for several months.

METHOD

1 Peel and core the apples and cook them to a pulp
   over a very low heat with a few tablespoons of water
   to prevent burning. Keep the lid on the pan, but look
   occasionally to see that there is enough water.

2 When the apples are soft and mashed smooth, add
   the butter and stir till melted. (The other half of the
   packet of unsalted butter can be used for making
   Biscuit Apricot Pie, page 154.)

3 Add the juice and grated rind of the lemons.

4 Stir in the sugar.

5 Add the beaten eggs.

6 Cook over a gentle heat. Stir constantly and patiently
   until the curd really thickens – each bubble leaves a
   momentary 'crater'.

7 Pot into clean jars and cover with waxed discs and
   paper circles as for jam.

Cranberry Jam

This is a jam to make at Christmas time when most of
the jam-making fruit has gone. It makes a pleasant
change from marmalade. As it only takes a little cooking,
it keeps best in the refrigerator.

Makes approximately 2 lb. jam

INGREDIENTS

1 lb. fresh cranberries   1 lb granulated sugar
1 pint water

METHOD

1   Remove stalks from cranberries, wash and pick over
    the fruit. Put in the preserving pan or a large sauce-
    pan with the water and simmer till the cranberries
    pop and are broken down.

2   Add the sugar, stir over low heat until sugar is dis-
    solved, then boil rapidly till setting point is reached
    (drops should fall in lazy flakes from a wooden spoon;
    or a temperature of 220°F is reached; or the jam sets
    when a little is cooled on a saucer).

3   Pot and cover.

Seville Jelly*

The time-consuming part of marmalade-making is the
shredding of the peel. In this recipe there is no shredding
because one aims for a clear, sparkling jelly, without peel.
It does not set very firmly at first but stiffens a little with
keeping. For full flavour use genuine Seville oranges, not
just ordinary 'bitters'.

✳ Seville oranges may be frozen whole or at the roughly cut
  stage. The rest of the method can be completed at any time
  of the year. Thaw completely first.

Roughly cut up Sevilles and simmer them with water and lemon juice. Then strain for several hours or overnight through a jelly bag. Simmer the strained liquid with sugar till setting point is reached.

Yield: 5 lb. – it sets best if potted in small jars

INGREDIENTS

2 lb. Seville oranges
4 pints water
juice of 2 lemons

3 lb. sugar
glycerine or butter

METHOD

1   Roughly cut up the scrubbed oranges (each one into about 8 pieces) and place, complete with all pips and pith, in the pan. Add 3 pints of the water and the lemon juice. Place the lid on the pan and simmer for 2 hours.

2   Strain through a scalded jelly bag (or two clean tea towels machined together round the edges and taped at the corners).

3   After it has dripped for 20 minutes, return the cooked fruit to the pan and simmer with the last pint of water for a further 20 minutes.

4   Re-strain through the jelly bag, allowing it to drip undisturbed for several hours or overnight.

5   Rub the rinsed and dried preserving pan with glycerine or butter to prevent foaming. Pour the strained liquid into the pan and simmer a little if it looks rather thin.

6   Add the sugar and stir over a low heat till dissolved.

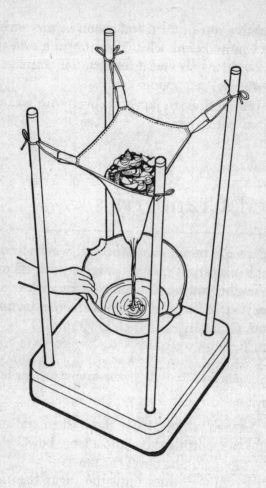

Boil hard till setting point is reached just as you do
for jams or marmalades. (One test is: put a small
spoonful on a saucer, allow to cool in a refrigerator
if possible. When ready to pot, the cold sample
wrinkles when pushed with a finger.) A tip: for an

alternative test put a metal spoon in the refrigerator while you make the jelly. To test, put a *little* jelly on the ice-cold spoon and if ready it will wrinkle almost immediately.

7   Pour into hot, clean jars and cover with waxed discs and jam-pot covers.

Stirred Cranberries

This is a recipe popular in Norway, where fresh cranberries are snipped in half with the scissors, then stirred with sugar until the sugar melts. Serve with cream, ice cream, yogurt, fruit salad, breakfast cereal or on bread and butter. Cranberries are rich in vitamin C.

INGREDIENTS

1 lb. fresh cranberries   9 oz. granulated sugar

METHOD

1   With kitchen scissors, halve the washed and stemmed cranberries, cutting them into a large bowl.
2   Stir in the sugar and cover the bowl.
3   Stir every 15 minutes until the sugar has melted – about 2 hours.
4   Transfer berries and sugar to covered jars.

Keeps 1 week at even temperature, 2 weeks in a cold larder, or 4 weeks or longer in a refrigerator.

Quick Raspberry Jam

This jam is more like a conserve as it does not set very firmly. It has a delicious full flavour because there is no added water and the cooking time is minimal. Bring the raspberries gently to the boil and boil rapidly for 5 minutes. Add the warmed sugar, stir to dissolve and boil rapidly for 1 minute. Skim and pot.

Yield: 5 lb.

INGREDIENTS

2½ lb. fresh raspberries   butter or glycerine
3 lb. granulated sugar

METHOD

1 Hull and pick over the raspberries but do not wash unless absolutely necessary. If you do wash them, drain them very thoroughly a few at a time in a sieve.
2 Put the sugar to warm in a cool oven.
3 Grease the preserving pan with a little butter or glycerine to prevent foaming later. Bring the fruit gently to the boil, without any water, then boil rapidly for 5 minutes.
4 Remove from the heat, add the sugar and stir well over low heat until all the sugar has dissolved.
5 Bring to the boil and boil rapidly for 1 minute only.
6 Skim quickly, pour jam at once into dry, warm jars and cover.

Weights and Measures

LIQUID MEASURES

British

1 quart	=	2 pints	=	40 fluid oz.
1 pint	=	4 gills	=	20 fl. oz.
½ pint	=	2 gills or one cup	=	10 fl. oz.
¼ pint	=	8 tablespoons	=	5 fl. oz.
		1 tablespoon	=	just over ½ fl. oz.
		1 dessertspoon	=	⅓ fl. oz.
		1 teaspoon	=	⅙ fl. oz.

Metric

1 litre = 10 decilitres (dl) = 100 centilitres (cl) = 1000 millilitres (ml).

Approximate equivalents

BRITISH	METRIC
1 quart	1·1 litres
1 pint	6 dl
½ pint	3 dl
¼ pint (1 gill)	1·5 dl
1 tablespoon	15 ml
1 dessertspoon	10 ml
1 teaspoon	5 ml

METRIC	BRITISH
1 litre	35 fl. oz.
$\frac{1}{2}$ litre (5 dl)	18 fl. oz.
$\frac{1}{4}$ litre (2.5 dl)	9 fl. oz.
1 dl	$3\frac{1}{2}$ fl. oz.

American

1 quart	=	2 pints	=	32 fl. oz.
1 pint	=	2 cups	=	16 fl. oz.
		1 cup	=	8 fl. oz.
		1 tablespoon	=	$\frac{1}{3}$ fl. oz.
		1 teaspoon	=	$\frac{1}{6}$ fl. oz.

Approximate equivalents

BRITISH	AMERICAN
1 quart	$2\frac{1}{2}$ pints
1 pint	$1\frac{1}{4}$ pints
$\frac{1}{2}$ pint	10 fl. oz. ($1\frac{1}{4}$ cups)
$\frac{1}{4}$ pint (1 gill)	5 fl. oz.
1 tablespoon	$1\frac{1}{2}$ tablespoons
1 dessertspoon	1 tablespoon
1 teaspoon	$\frac{1}{3}$ fl. oz.

AMERICAN	BRITISH
1 quart	$\frac{1}{2}$ pint + 3 tbs (32 fl. oz.)
1 pint	$\frac{3}{4}$ pint + 2 tbs (16 fl. oz.)
1 cup	$\frac{1}{2}$ pint − 2 tbs (8 fl. oz.)

SOLID MEASURES

British
16 oz. = 1 lb.

Metric
1000 grammes = 1 kilogramme

Approximate equivalents

BRITISH	METRIC
1 lb. (16 oz.)	400 grammes
$\frac{1}{2}$ lb. (8 oz.)	200 g
$\frac{1}{4}$ lb. (4 oz.)	100 g
1 oz.	25 g

METRIC	BRITISH
1 kilo (1000 g)	2 lb. 3 oz.
$\frac{1}{2}$ kilo (500 g)	1 lb. 2 oz.
$\frac{1}{4}$ kilo (250 g)	9 oz.
100 g	$3\frac{1}{2}$ oz.

Equivalent Oven Temperatures

°Fahrenheit	Gas	°Centigrade
225°F	Mark ¼	110°C Very cool
250°F	½	130°C Very cool
275°F	1	140°C Cool
300°F	2	150°C Cool
325°F	3	170°C Moderate
350°F	4	180°C Moderate
375°F	5	190°C Fairly hot
400°F	6	200°C Fairly hot
425°F	7	220°C Hot
450°F	8	230°C Very hot
475°F	9	240°C Very hot

List of Illustrations

Index

More about Penguins and Pelicans

Penguinews, which appears every month, contains details of all the new books issued by Penguins as they are published. From time to time it is supplemented by *Penguins in Print*, which is a complete list of all titles available. (There are some five thousand of these.)

A specimen copy of *Penguinews* will be sent to you free on request. For a year's issues (including the complete lists) please send 50p if you live in the British Isles, or 75p if you live elsewhere. Just write to Dept EP, Penguin Books Ltd, Harmondsworth, Middlesex, enclosing a cheque or postal order, and your name will be added to the mailing list.

In the U.S.A.: For a complete list of books available from Penguin in the United States write to Dept CS, Penguin Books Inc., 7110 Ambassador Road, Baltimore, Maryland 21207.

In Canada: For a complete list of books available from Penguin in Canada write to Penguin Books Canada Ltd, 41 Steelcase Road West, Markham, Ontario.

a Penguin Handbook

The Beginner's Cookery Book

Betty Falk

The Beginner's Cookery Book began life as an extremely successful handbook for teenagers. For this version the author has expanded and adapted the text for aspiring cooks of any age who want to make a good job of meals without too much culinary fuss.

Mrs Falk provides here over 150 recipes for dishes which are easy to make and eat, and look good. They range from Green Salad to Sole Meunière and include nourishing soups, egg dishes, fish and meat sauces, vegetables and puddings: there are chapters on cakes, pastries and jams, as well as 'Drinks That Don't Come Out of a Bottle'. Betty Falk also makes suggestions for party menus, and includes a list of cooking utensils, a glossary of terms and advice on dietetic values.

In its present guise her book offers invaluable aid to those who are progressing beyond the bacon-and-egg stage.

a Penguin Handbook

Left Over for Tomorrow

Marika Hanbury Tenison

'Leftovers for me form the backbone of my daily family cooking and also the basis for many of my favourite dinner party dishes. . . . Without leftovers my housekeeping bills would soar and I would lose a large portion of the fun and satisfaction I get from cooking and experimenting with food.' So writes the author in her foreword, and this remarkable book contains over 200 recipes – not only quick non-fuss meals for the benefit of the busy bachelor, but also some very sophisticated culinary adventures.

Amongst the recipes given are Fish and Anchovy Ramekins, Consommé Julienne, Fisherman's Pie, Lamb in Rich Orange Sauce, Ham Mimosa, West Indian Mashed Potatoes, American Muffins, Tipsy Trifle and Frosted Grapes.

Marika Hanbury Tenison has also written *Soups and Hors d'Oeuvres* for Penguin Handbooks, has contributed articles to many magazines and newspapers, and is now the cookery editor of the *Sunday Telegraph*.

a Penguin Handbook

The Pauper's Cookbook

Jocasta Innes

Jocasta Innes dreamed of a cookery book planned for church mice. 'What greedy paupers needed above all, I felt, was a book where all the recipes were nice enough to be tempting, but so cheap they would be painlessly trained to economize.' But no other indigent expert came forward to write it: so she has written it herself.

In *The Pauper's Cookbook* she has assembled a wealth (or should it be a poverty?) of recipes for meals costing between ten and twenty pence per head. Her collection of international, racially mixed and classless dishes promises good home cooking at 'Joe's Café' prices.

Some of the worst cooks waste hours on research: but *The Pauper's Cookbook* bypasses all that. You simply assess the 'cooking situation' and turn up the recommended treatment. The Ffortescue-Smyths – or your parents – might call for Fancy Work; young Tomlinson and his dolly-bird, Fast Work; but the Joneses and all those children of theirs come in for Standards and Padding, including reconditioned leftovers. Thrifty tips on Programmed Eating (a week's meals at one session), on not eating (or dieting), and on Private Enterprise (or make-it-yourself) help to cut the costs; and Jocasta Innes starts right where the trouble begins – in the shops.

So leave it to the affluent to court indigestion at the Waldorf-Ritz: here's how to live it up your in own squalid tenement without recourse to poaching, rustling, guddling, scrumping or shop-lifting.

a Penguin Handbook

Easy Cooking for One or Two

Louise Davies

If you are cooking for one or two, this is the book for you. Most cookery books cater for four or more: for smaller numbers you are often left to choose between wasteful, expensive dishes and a boring, unsound diet. But here Louise Davies solves your problem with over 150 easy, enjoyable recipes in small quantities.

Her first chapter gives valuable tips on nourishing foods, whilst the second contains ideas for those who need to keep well with the minimum of cooking effort or who have never had to cook before. Subsequent chapters contain progressively more adventurous recipes and at the end there are useful hints on storing food.

Easy Cooking for One or Two has been written mostly with the 'Over-60s' in mind: for this reason all the ideas in the book (which is printed in large type for easy reference) have been tested and approved by 'Over-60s' and 'Retirement' cookery students throughout the country.

'An excellent guide to maximum nutrition at minimum expense of both money and effort' – Catherine Stott in the *Guardian*

'The book is excellent, the recipes are cheap, easy to make even if you can't cook' – Sheila Hutchins in the *Daily Express*

Not for sale in the U.S.A.